Let the Prophets Speak

Commissioning and Calling Forth the New Guard

Volume 1

Vincom Publishing Co.
Tulsa, Oklahoma

Unless otherwise indicated, all Scripture quotations are taken from the *King James Version* of the Bible.

All Scripture quotations marked NIV are taken from *The Holy Bible: New International Version*. Copyright © 1973, 1978, 1984 by The International Bible Society. Used by permission of Zondervan Bible Publishers.

All Greek and Hebrew words and definitions are from *Strong's Exhaustive Concordance*, by James Strong. (Grand Rapids: Baker Book House, 1982.)

Let the Prophets Speak
Commissioning and Calling Forth the New Guard
ISBN 0-927936-90-9
Copyright © 1996 by
Vincom Publishing Co.
P. O. Box 702160
Tulsa, OK 74170

Published by Vincom Publishing Co.
P. O. Box 702160
Tulsa, OK 74170
(918) 254-1276

Contents

Foreword by Carlton Pearson

I was born and reared in the Church of God in Christ; I am a fourth generation, classical Pentecostal preacher, including my maternal great-grandfather, my paternal grandfather, and my own father. I've never been afraid of a prophet or prophecy, but the presence of prophets was scarce, both in the church in which I grew up, and throughout the denomination at large.

Those few daring souls who were considered prophets were looked upon with a fair or unfair amount of suspicion, depending on how you looked at it. I think that attitude probably carried over into my present-day appraisal of prophets and/or prophecy in the Church. There has been much conversation, and not a small amount of controversy, throughout the Body of Christ concerning the function, the office and the presence of prophecy and its efficacy or necessity in the modern church.

Both non-Charismatic and Charismatic/Pentecostal groups have debated, not so much over prophecy as "prophets." Christians overall have always had a fascination with end-of-the-world predictions, eschatological, or apocalyptic teachings, books and lectures. Within Charismatic circles, an occasional or even frequent "message in tongues" and/or its interpretation within a church service has been widely received throughout most of this century, with greater or lesser acceptance, depending sometimes on the season or even the geographical region.

However, when it comes to the subject of "prophets" within the house, most of us have strong apprehension and even doctrinal disputations. A word of knowledge or wisdom, discerning of spirits, gifts of healings, and even miracles have received fairly wide acceptance. Again, however — a prophet? A prophet has more trouble being accepted than even an "apostle"; and apostles have had and continue to have their share of cynics.

After a long and prayerful re-appraisal and observation of the function, along with a scriptural study of its authenticity, I've come to the conclusion that the Body of Christ has been largely operating from a three-fingered hand. With the Biblically ordained five-fold ministry, as recorded in Ephesians 4:11, I see the "apostle" as the thumb, which touches all of the gifts; the "prophet" as the forefinger, warning the people to repent; the "evangelist" as the long, middle finger, wooing and inviting people into the Kingdom; the "pastor" as the ring finger of commitment (the unbroken circle); and the "teacher" as the little finger that digs into the deeper secrets of the truth.

In the Old Testament, when the land was in famine and drought, the most famous prophet, Elijah, heard the sound of the abundance of rain coming from a cloud about the size of a man's hand. I see that as being a figurative expression of the Church in the modern world with the hand of God in operation, the five-fingered hand of God: Apostle, prophet, evangelist, pastor and teacher. I think he was prophesying about the Church of the New Testament, with all the fingers of God in operation.

When the New Testament prophet, John the Baptist, came preaching "in the wilderness" (desert), there had been no word from God for over 400 years.

Yet the priests read from the scrolls every Sabbath. They had the word *of* God, but they didn't have a word *from* God. For so many years our churches have been experiencing — as the Scripture says — "a famine in the land for the Word of God."

Ephesians 2:19,20 NIV says, **Consequently, you are no longer foreigners and aliens, but fellow citizens with God's people and members of God's household, built on the *foundation* of the apostles and prophets, with Christ Jesus himself as the chief cornerstone.**

If, in fact, the household of God is built on the foundation of the apostles and prophets, why have we played down the ministry of apostleship and/or the prophet? Why are we so afraid of the function of those two Biblical offices? I believe this fear is part of a satanic and diabolical conspiracy. The correction of abuse is not necessarily disuse. I realize there has been some abuse of the office of a prophet or the function of an apostle in some instances, but we must still honor the gifts of God as He ordained them Biblically.

I believe that as you read this book with the probing discernment of the Holy Spirit, you will discover a very intelligent appraisal of the function, office, and anointing on the prophet. I know my mind as a pastor has been broadened through my acceptance and openness to the ministry of prophecy and the prophet in my local church. We don't have excesses here, but there will always be wildfire or strange fire mixed with the true fire. However, by the discernment of the Holy Ghost, we can know the difference. We need that fire. I am not afraid of the wildfire. It is the strange fire that concerns me — that fire that cannot be identified as pertaining to the Scriptures or to the holiness of God. This book will help you know the difference.

I highly recommend this book to you with an open heart and an open mind with firm approach and commendation of the men and women who speak here and what they have to say. I pray that it will bless your life as it has my life and my church. If pastors accept what God says about the office of an apostle and a prophet — and their function as it relates to the New Testament Church of this particular dispensation — then their churches will no longer operate by a three-fingered hand, but by the five-fingered hand of God in full operation. The hand of God is moving, and we're the fulfillment of the cloud that Elijah saw for rain to fall on the land in famine and drought.

There is a true latter rain about to fall again as we close this decade, close this century, and close this millennium. God bless you as you hear and "Let the Prophets Speak!"

Part One
Commissioned to Greatness

by Pam Vinnett

1

Five Tenets of a Commissioned Life

To be *commissioned* means to be issued written papers giving certain powers or privileges; to be given a warrant or license; or written orders giving rank or authority as an officer in the armed forces.

Many Christians do not understand that we are not only called, but chosen, or *commissioned* by God, called, so to speak, into His vast army. As a Church, corporately, all believers have been given a general commission, referred to as "The Great Commission" (usually quoted from Mark 16:15-18), but commissioning speaks of much more.

Some are "commissioned" as officers in the Body: apostles, prophets, evangelists, teachers, and pastors. Other specific commissions may involve the field of music, business, or administration of church and ministry affairs. But the important thing to remember is that each commission is an order from above which should not be ignored or taken lightly.

As one called to the office of prophet, I have observed five significant characteristics that operate in the lives of those who carry out their divine commissions wholeheartedly. All of us are *commissioned to greatness*, but not all will achieve it. Mediocrity is usually the result of laxity in one or all of these five areas. Failure is the outcome of ignoring them completely.

3

The first tenet of a person whose heart is after God's is *purity of purpose*. God's love is more than hugs and cheek kisses to saints and lip service to God during praise and worship. It is not based on sentimentality. True love issues from the core of your being and laces all you do if you are pure.

The present generation thinks love means allowing them to do whatever they please no matter the consequences. The fact that real love also disciplines is not a part of their awareness. The last two moves of God have involved people whose world views begin with this definition of love.

In fact, the Charismatic movement was wonderful because the knowledge that God loves us needed to be restored to the Church. However, it did not include within it the tantamount importance of sanctification. Previous generations knew being saved was only the beginning, but conversion involved the daily tempering which yields the fruit of a Christlike nature in us. (2 Corinthians 3:18.)

Sad to say, since World War II a large portion of the Church in America has taught that becoming saved is all there is to the Christian life. There is much teaching that a new nature is God's gift which we have absolutely nothing to do with improving or causing to grow. There is very little teaching that, as a new creature, we have certain responsibilities to become like our Head, Jesus.

Purity means "to be free from whatever is evil," and "to purge, or to purify, the heart from ungodly characteristics." God can freely move through a heart that is pure, having no ulterior motives bending or stretching it toward anything but Him.

King David, for example, in spite of his adulterous

liaison, murder of Bathsheba's husband, and failure to bring up his children right, was "a man after God's own heart." (1 Samuel 13:14; Acts 13:22.) That does not mean God ignored his sin or that God is like David. It means that David "followed after" God's heart through submission to His will and repentance.

In spite of his mistakes and major sins, David had purity of purpose toward God.

The second tenet is to learn that *your own righteousness is not righteousness at all.* The more you seek to "press in" to the Father, studying His Word, the more you will start to understand, as Isaiah did, that you have no righteousness outside of Jesus Christ. (Isaiah 6:5, 64:6; Romans 3:21,22.) Our righteousness as believers is only through the Kingdom of God. *Christ is the Righteousness of God*

The third tenet is to totally *lose the fear of failure.* If you are afraid of going forward, you will never do anything great for God. Every obstacle that can hit you is going to hit you. *no weapon formed against you shall prosper* You must know beyond the shadow of a doubt that all things are possible with God (Luke 1:37), and that all things do not *have* to be possible with you. You will never succeed in your own strength, but in His.

It is not who you know (have knowledge of); it is who you *know* (enjoy intimacy with). If there is no true intimate relationship with Him, you will never become great or make His name great in the earth. *Love — Prophetic*

Number four is *faith*, one of the most misused, misunderstood words in the Bible. Too many Christians are void of understanding when it comes to faith. We have heard a lot of teaching on faith in the past twenty years. However, somehow, a majority only "heard" that faith means confessing a thing until you get it. There is much more to faith than that.

Hebrews 11:1 says, **Now faith is the substance of things hoped for, the evidence of things not seen.**

That verse says much more than we usually are taught in our churches. This is not merely referring to faith as "a force" similar to "The Force" in the movie, *Star Wars*. This exclusive belief can open the door to the operation of witchcraft and the occult, rather than real faith.

Faith is not a force alone. The Greek literally says that faith is *the title deed* to things you hope to receive but that you have not seen yet. Faith simplistically is believing something is absolutely true, whether you comprehend how it is true or not.

If you "know that you know" God never lies and that His promises are true, you can present your faith as a title deed to receive whatever God has promised. Notice, I said *whatever God has promised*, not whatever you arbitrarily decide you want.

Finally, the last tenet is *to be aware of your divine commission*. It is very important to know your specific commission. Too many are called as foot soldiers, but think they are generals. Consequently, they make terrible, useless generals, never achieving the work of good foot soldiers.

If you are called as a foot soldier, be the greatest foot soldier you can be. Don't covet the general's position. If you knew what that actually entails, you would not desire it anyway! Be thrilled to not have the responsibility or accountability of a general.

When rewards are delegated, you will not be judged in comparison to another. God's rewards are based solely upon how faithful and obedient you were in carrying out your own commission.

If your feet are a size 12, and the general's boots are size 12, you may fit them, but they will not make you a general. Only God can make a general in His Kingdom. Not only that, the enemy who sees you in the general's boots will shoot at you as if you *were* the general. The enemy shoots to kill, and you would not have a general's defenses.

Whoever you are, wherever God has placed you in the Body, it is important to be in that place. Being in the right place is of critical importance to your divine commission.

Let's explore these five tenets in more depth in the next few chapters.

Love

but Prophetic Voice Apostle Owarn, Eric My eternal Kings though art a General to the Apostolic & Prophetic Movements at once, with the latter, enjoy the adventure, with God.

2
Purity of Purpose

A good example of someone in the Bible with purity of heart and purpose is Mary, the mother of Jesus. The first thing we are shown concerning her is her *purity.*

Scholars of culture in Jewish history tell us that she was probably only about fifteen years old when she received the greatest commission of all. Imagine a teenager being given the responsibility by God to bear and rear His Son!

To be chosen, Mary had to be pure in body, and her response to the angel who brought her commission shows us she also was pure in mind and heart. What we know of her life shows us that her purity of heart allowed, or caused, her to operate in purity of purpose concerning her assignment.

Gabriel, the messenger of God, had been sent to the nation of Judah to announce the birth of John the Baptist. (Luke 1:13-26.) About six months later, he made another momentous trip to the earth. He was sent to a virgin in Galilee, a country adjacent to Judah, to a young girl already betrothed to a man named Joseph.

> **And the angel came in unto her, and said, Hail, thou that art highly favoured, the Lord is with thee: blessed art thou among women. And when she saw him, she was troubled at his saying, and cast in her mind what manner of salutation this should be. And**

9

**the angel said unto her, Fear not, Mary: for thou hast
found favour with God. And, behold, thou shalt
conceive in thy womb, and bring forth a son, and shalt
call his name JESUS.**

Luke 1:28-31

We should notice that God did not send the angel
to correct Mary's wearing apparel or religious concepts.
He went straight to the issue of her commission and
allowed her walk with Him to correct anything not
pleasing to Him.

God knew her heart, and He chose her out of all of
the virgins available in her generation. He did not come
to perfect her on the outside, He came to empower her
on the inside.

Mary probably had heard the prophecy of Isaiah
concerning the promised Messiah much of her life.
(Isaiah 7:14.) Isaiah had written more than 700 years
previously that one day a virgin would conceive and
bear a son who would save God's people.

We are hearing a lot about angelic visitations these
days. Unfortunately, most of what we hear is not from
God but psychic apparitions. I would imagine this true
angelic visitation to Mary must have been very startling,
considering Gabriel's visit was totally unexpected. I
doubt if anyone in her village had ever seen an angel.

The Bible says that Mary only asked one very
crucial question, **How shall this be, seeing I know not
a man?** (v. 34.)

God answered, "That is all right, Mary. I have it all
taken care of. The Holy Thing to be conceived within
you shall be called the Son of God."

**And Mary said, Behold the handmaid of the
Lord; be it unto me according to thy word. And the
angel departed from her.**

Luke 1:38

In addition to knowing that she was pure of heart because God chose her, we can see purity of heart in her response to Gabriel. This was in total contrast to how Gabriel dealt with the priest Zacharias six months before. Angels in the Bible react, or respond, to the heart motivation of a person.

Zacharias asked a similar kind of question when told that he and Elizabeth, both old, were going to have a son. Gabriel promptly said he had unbelief, not a pure heart of faith, striking him dumb until John's birth. (Luke 1:18-20.) Why was God so hard on him? Being a priest, he should have been well versed in the law as well as God's ways. When he entered the holy place, he should have expected God to show up and speak. Instead, he was fearful and questioned God's validity and ability. This was a costly lesson.

Purity of Heart Does Not Eliminate Trouble

If you know you are called to greatness, do not think that just because you laid down selfish ambition and said, "Yes, Lord, impregnate me with Your purpose," everything is going to go smoothly. Mary went through trouble and anguish of heart from the moment she accepted God's will.

She was suspected of having committed adultery.

She had to make a hard journey in the last stages of pregnancy and give birth in a stable of beast.

She had to flee to Egypt for fear her baby would be killed and be exiled from her family and home for several years.

Finally, she saw her firstborn son reviled and then crucified, an anguish few mothers could bear. However, her purity of purpose, along with the other four tenets mentioned, caused her to have strength through the difficult, painful times.

Why do we think trouble can be confessed away, blamed on others, or only comes as a result of demonic intervention? If God has impregnated you with a divine commission, He will often "trouble" your fleshly path to get you on His divine path.

When you are commissioned, you can be certain that trouble will come. Some will be an attack from the enemy, some from circumstances, but some because of your commission. God calls you, and then works on you to get you prepared to fulfill your call.

A certain "S" word is considered a "four-letter" word in some segments of the Church today. That word is suffering. You will go through some things when you are pregnant with a vision from God, but remember the angel said, "The Holy Ghost is going to take care of it! What are you worried about? Trust God."

Ezekiel 14:2-4 tells us what happens when the intentions of the heart are not pure.

> **And the word of the Lord came unto me, saying, Son of man, these men have set up their idols in their heart, and put the stumblingblock of their iniquity before their face: should I be enquired of at all by them? Therefore speak unto them, and say unto them, Thus saith the Lord God; Every man of the house of Israel that setteth up his idols in his heart, and putteth the stumblingblock of his iniquity before his face, and cometh to the prophet; I the Lord will answer him that cometh *according to the multitude of his idols*.**

I am indebted to Dr. Paula Price for causing me to see this concept and to think along these lines. God gave Ezekiel a twofold warning for the Israelites living in Babylonian bondage: He will speak according to the kind of idolatry and according to the number of idols in your heart.

God has always used His prophets to deliver words of warning and judgment. It has been erroneously taught that God does not use New Testament prophets for this purpose (judgments), but that is not true. The New Testament word for *prophet* as found in Ephesians 4:11, which is the Greek word *prophetes*, includes in its meaning all of the attributes, powers and abilities of the Old Testament prophet, but with a better covenant. If the New Testament prophet gives a judgment call from God, God will back him or her up with His commissioned orders. God is not in the business of fortune-telling or giving words with which we readily agree. Likewise, we are not given the option of trying to see to it that the words spoken come to pass by our own actions.

When we get into these things, idolatry can result. In order to have the stipulations outlined in the Ezekiel reference happen to you, you must become obsessed with the issue of your heart regardless of whether it is God's desire for you.

Be Careful: You May Get What You Pray for!

Let me give an example. A young man sees a pretty girl and says to himself, "I wish I could date that girl." He then begins to think, dream and fantasize about her day and night.

Then he says, "I really believe God wants me to get to know her."

He asks her out for a date, and she turns him down. But our young man will not take no for an answer. After all, he knows how to get God to do things for him! He has "faith."

So he goes into his prayer closet and prays, "God, I know You want me to have this young woman. Turn her heart toward me. To confirm it, have her to look in my direction. I want her to love me and become my wife. I just know this is Your will."

As he prays those soulish prayers that really amount to witchcraft, it is possible that pretty soon, he may have someone prophesy to him, "God spoke to me that a certain young woman is supposed to be your wife, and God will save her to give her to you!" That young man may even receive precisely what he "confessed and believed" for, getting with the marriage the penalties and unhappiness of marriage to an unbeliever, or one who is simply not suited for his life's purpose.

God warns us that if we keep seeking Him with obsessions and idols in our hearts, He Himself will speak to us according to them. We do not want to even consider the possibility of the thing happening to us that God told Ezekiel He would do to those with impure hearts:

> ...I the Lord will answer him by myself: And I will set my face against that man, and will make him a sign and a proverb, and I will cut him off from the midst of my people; and ye shall know that I am the Lord.
>
> **Ezekiel 14:7,8**

Also, the prophet who is deceived and gives false prophecies is in big trouble as well! (Ezekiel 14:9,10.)

Purity makes good ground for the promised seed to be planted, then birthed in your heart by God's fatherhood. An impure heart is a festering ground for idolatrous relationships, attracting people who are also impure.

Christians with idols in their heart, seeking God to

obtain those things, may attract prophets whose desire is for recognition and money. Like attracts like, or as the old saying goes, "Birds of a feather flock together."

Indications of an Impure Heart

In addition to greed and ambition, there are a number of other indications of an impure heart with wrong motives. One is pride; another is rebellion to authority. In fact, pride, rebellion, and self-will are the core of Satan's heart imparted to Adam and Eve and inherited by all human beings. (Genesis 3:1-7; Isaiah 14:12-14.)

Someone with a pure heart has been cleansed of these unrighteous characteristics and is set single-mindedly toward doing the will of God.

Michal, daughter of King Saul and one of the wives of King David, had her womb shut up because of the impurity of her heart. When Israel recaptured the Ark of the Covenant after some seventy years, and it was being returned to Jerusalem in a triumphal parade, Michal got into trouble.

She saw her husband leading a parade of dancers and singers praising God because the ark had finally come back to its proper resting place. David was dancing and glorifying God with all of his might and had thrown off his kingly garments as a sign of praise, honor and humility before God. God was so pleased with David's heart and attitude that He honored him.

However, Michal said, "Look at my man out there showing his body to all those women," and despised him in her heart for being undignified as befitted a king. Unfortunately, she not only thought ill of David, but out of the abundance of her heart, her big mouth spoke. God punished her by shutting up her womb. (2 Samuel 6:12-23.)

As I speak to bodies of believers all over the world, I find myself stressing the importance of respect for authorities. Authorities in the Church are not to be corrected from the pews, but from above.

God has order in His Kingdom. God regiments His Kingdom greater and better than the kingdoms of men. All authority in government comes from God. He does not dictate the kind of governmental system, nor does He sovereignly put every person in office. People have their rights to choose in countries where the governing system allows that.

However, God ordains order, and once you are in office, your heart is in His hand because the principle of governing offices is His. (Romans 13:1.) Furthermore, God will often see to it that certain officials gain office just to be used to punish mankind, as with Israel's first king, Saul. We may choose but God ordains for His purposes. You cannot find a greater order for how to run a nation, than that which God gave Moses in the wilderness to govern three million rebellious Israelites.

If you compare the Church to the U. S. military authority, you would have the president, then generals as the highest authorities, followed by other ranking officials. Everyone knows foot soldiers do not correct generals. However, when it comes to correcting God's generals, we are void of understanding protocol.

Many Christians feel they can make an appointment with an apostle, prophet, pastor, etc. or write a letter and straighten them out. That is not the order of God. If each Christian put every effort into working the position in which God has placed him or her, there would not be time left in which to erroneously correct or criticize others. There is enough work for each of us.

Purity of heart and purpose will not "buck" God's properly constituted authority but will pray about situations and let "the Boss" handle them Himself.

3

His Righteousness and None of Your Own

The number two tenet is righteousness consciousness. David, whose name means "well beloved," was a champion of God. However, one year when all of the kings went out to battle, David decided to remain in Jerusalem. (2 Samuel 11:1.)

He was out on his roof sightseeing when he should have been on the battlefield. That is a very, very important point. If God has an appointed place for you, that is the "now" place for you. If you are out of place and out of sync, you can literally miss the blessing of the Lord.

David was out of place by tarrying in Jerusalem. He saw a woman named Bathsheba bathing naked, sent for her, lay with her, and conceived a child. Then he contrived a scheme to put Uriah the Hittite, her husband, out on the battlefield, so that he would be killed. David was not conscious of his righteousness in God. Temptation and failure were the results.

Look at what David lost for one night's indiscretion. He lost his first son by Bathsheba hours after his birth. He lost peace in his family and was rewarded with strife instead. As if that wasn't enough, insurrection and the sword repeatedly troubled his kingdom. Absalom,

19

his favorite son, as well as Adonijah, his fourth son, went into rebellion, attempting to overthrow his throne. Heartbreak, murder and calamity resulted.

God told David through Nathan, the prophet, exactly what losing his purity of heart would cost him.

> And I gave thee thy master's [Saul's] house, and thy master's wives into thy bosom, and gave thee the house of Israel and of Judah; and if that had been too little, I would moreover have given unto thee such and such things. Wherefore hast thou despised the commandment of the Lord, to do evil in his sight?... Now therefore the sword shall never depart from thine house; because thou hast despised me, and hast taken the wife of Uriah the Hittite to be thy wife. Thus saith the Lord, Behold, I will raise up evil against thee out of thine own house, and I will take thy wives before thine eyes, and give them unto thy neighbour, and he shall lie with thy wives in the sight of this sun. For thou didst it secretly: but I will do this thing before all Israel, and before the sun.
>
>   2 Samuel 12:8-12

Christians assume that this kind of consequence for sin was only an Old Testament event. After all, we live under the "covenant of grace," which means there are no harsh consequences for breaking covenant and sinning against a benevolent, loving God. I have news for you, the *New* Testament says the wages of sin is still death. However, the gift of God is eternal life in Christ Jesus.

Every true prophet, new and old, has one consistent message: They cry out against sin. That is because sin is the only thing that can separate you from God.

Many Christians going through difficulties presently are unaware that they either took a detour away from their purposes, or they are saying or doing something directly against the will of God. God's desire is not to instill guilt. It is to reinforce the understanding that we need the whole Bible.

We cannot take out what we think is nice, nor take out our favorite scripture and ignore the rest. We must never take the scriptures out of context or we will never become victorious.

Take, for example, the scripture, **And we know that all things work together for good....** This scripture is too often half quoted and taken out of context.

The first line of Romans 8:28 is not a general promise or principle. The Bible tells us specifically for whom all things work together for good. It is only for those who **love God, to them who are** *the* **called according to his purpose**.

We quote Isaiah 54:17, "No weapon formed against you shall prosper," and stop there. That promise is concerning the "heritage of the servants of the Lord," those whose righteousness is of Him. There are thousands of like scriptures of which we take the part and miss the whole.

If a starving man receives a whole loaf of bread, I guarantee that he will not leave a crumb behind. We must eat the whole loaf, realizing it is for our good. When God gives a "pill" of correction, swallow it even if it is bitter going down. It will make you well in the end.

Having His righteousness does not mean you can continue in sin and get away with it. That is "trampling the blood of Jesus under foot." (Hebrews 10:29.) You cannot earn His righteousness; it is a free gift as part of becoming a new creature. (2 Corinthians 5:17.) However, we are to "conform" to His image (righteousness) through submission to His will, His Word and His way. Nevertheless, Lord, not my will, but your will be done. (Luke 22:42.)

4

Boldness and Faith

A third essential principle of those commissioned to greatness is the lack of fear of failure, which results in divine boldness. People who become great in God are willing to step out in faith and not become paralyzed, even if they stumble or err. They understand that they must repent immediately, correct the error and continue moving forward.

The Apostle Paul was such a man. Despite being beaten, maligned, shipwrecked and imprisoned, Paul was never diverted from his purpose. He was so thoroughly dedicated to God that he did not miss his divine commissioning. But what did God do to get Paul's attention? He knocked him prostrate upon the Damascus road in front of officials and friends and blinded him to get him to see.

How many of us are still stumbling around in the dark room of our purpose today?

One of the most frequently asked questions I receive as a minister is, "Who am I (to God) and what am I called to do? Can you please tell me what God has for my life?"

Do you know why the psychic industry is a billion dollar industry? Because people are seeking direction, and they do not want to be accountable to God. They would rather pick up a phone and spend a small

23

fortune calling a psychic hotline, when they could come
to the house of God and receive His answers to all their
inquiries.

One woman allegedly spent $40,000 in a single
month calling psychics, and some may have spent more!
One chief of police in a small Arkansas town spent
$30,000 in one month calling psychics when the town
budget for the year was only $50,000. Obviously, he no
longer has a job, and the town is frantically hunting
ways to pay the bill — or to get out of paying it. People
desire instant gratification without accountability to
anyone, much less the Father.

If we really want to see what has been dubbed
the psychic age turn toward God and rightfully be
named the prophetic age, we must do it God's way. God
is judging the psychic hotline. You are going see them
being sued repeatedly. That is absolutely the word of
the Lord. In reality, Satan has once again done God
and His Church a tremendous favor! He has caused
curiosity concerning the supernatural to reach an
astounding height. When people who feel the ripeness
in the atmosphere become jaded with the emptiness that
comes as a result of seeking psychics, God's prophets
will be in position to answer their needs.

However, we must be aware that, whatever the
rationale is used for legally coming against psychics
will eventually be used also against the Church. Some
church counselors have already been sued when
people thought their advice ruined their lives instead
of helping. Persecution of this kind has always haunted
the Church, but we are growing stronger and more
capable through it. God will not be stopped!

Many Christians thought the Branch Davidian
debacle was acceptable because they were a "cult."

Legally, any group that says they are "the only way" can be classified as a cult. That episode was Satan's way of setting a precedent for the government to attack various churches and spiritual communities.

The point is that satanically influenced people are operating with great boldness today, while too many Christians attempt to carry out their commissions halfheartedly.

You must be willing to make mistakes. There is a huge difference between sinning and making honest mistakes. No one is perfect. We all stumble at some point along the way, just knowing we are right and then finding we were wrong. When this happens, we should never bullheadedly keep our stubborn stance, trying to find justification for our sin and failure. If you allow God to be Himself, He will show you that He is much bigger than your failures or inadequacies. He will deliver you.

Boldness in carrying out your commission and spreading the Gospel can bring you persecution and trials. But the difference is that if you get into trouble of your own accord, you are forced to acquire your own deliverance. However, if you get into difficulty for the sake of the Gospel, you have One fighting for you just like the fourth man in the fiery furnace of Nebuchadnazzar. (Daniel 3:25-27.) He will see that you come out not even smelling like smoke.

Faith Underwrites Everything

People frequently ask ministers, "How do you have faith?"

The fourth characteristic, *faith*, comes through relationship. If you have no relationship with God, you can have no faith in Him. If you do not spend time with the Divine Commissioner, having a personal relationship with Him, the Lord Jesus Christ, you will never have faith! You must study the Word of God, allowing it to work in and perfect His nature in you.

You can sit by a pond all day and confess, "I am a frog. I am a frog. I am a frog...," but you will never turn green and croak. You can only have faith in God if you know Him.

Anyone with whom I have an intimate relationship knows my voice and is seldom fooled by an alien voice. So it is with God. His sheep *know* His voice, and another they will not follow. (John 10:4,5.) After walking closely with God, He will develop within you the ability to respond to His every request. This is faith in its truest form, when you know that God said it or thought it, and in turn you act it out. You will never acquire this kind of Mark 11:22,23 faith by following at a distance. Intimacy alone gives birth to it.

Develop your faith by plugging in to Him Who has all of it. Put on the mind of Christ. Is that not what the Bible says? (1 Corinthians 2:16.)

How do you put on the mind of Christ? By exercising and cleaning up the corrupt mind, reprogramming your "computer" brain to speak His words, His will and act as He acts. (Romans 12:2.)

5
Awareness of Your Divine Commission

The final characteristic of those commissioned to greatness is awareness of their commissions. If you are unsure of who you are and in what direction you should be going, you must go to the Commissioner. He is the only One Who can answer you. I guarantee that, if you spend enough time with Him, you will automatically know what He has commissioned you to do.

If we spent as much time with God as we do with people in fellowship on the phone or otherwise, no one would be wondering, "Who am I?" and "What am I called to do?"

If God commissioned you, the Holy Ghost has already impregnated you, but your baby will be still-born if you do not connect yourself to the Source and get the power to deliver. You must "eat right" spiritually so that what is planted in you can grow whole and not be malnourished or malformed. Also, you will never give birth if you are not willing to sacrifice and suffer for the birth. There is, of necessity, a spiritual travail that precedes every spiritual birth. Please remember, the Holy Spirit has no children on welfare. Those He fathers are richly cared for by Him.

This is the time for the Body of Christ to become aware of its commission to unify as never before in the history of the American church. We will see persecution of the Church (especially in this country) as we have never seen it hitherto. Presently, there is plotting behind closed doors concerning how to prevent Christians from having any input into government affairs. Further, there are forces that desire to destroy the financial base of God's house. But to be forewarned is to be forearmed.

I prophesied over ten years ago that the IRS was going to rise up against churches and ministries, and there would be all kinds of turbulence and problems. I saw preachers being arrested and jailed. If you are a Christian businessman or businesswoman, an individual, or ministry who handles money in any capacity, be prepared to be audited, checked, and double-checked.

When the IRS pursued us, I said to God, "Who are we to incur such blatant harassment? We are not even rich."

Then the Holy Spirit responded, "It is not who you are in the natural but who you are in the Kingdom."

Many Christians already are being persecuted in money matters because of who they are to the Kingdom. Do not take it personally, but get your books in order. Leave no hole through which the devil can shoot his fiery darts.

And when they revile you and persecute you and say all manner of things against you, just know that you have come into great company. Officials and religious leaders did the same both to Jesus and to the prophets who preceded you! (Matthew 5:11,12.)

I admonish my students often by asking them, "Do you know that it is all right not to be liked?" I adjure them to live to please God and He will take care of them.

A prophet's life is not one of popularity or popular notoriety. Everyone will not like them, nor should they be liked always. People may seemingly love you today for what you prophesy and despise you tomorrow. Prophets are used by God as "scouring pads" to gain access to the inside of your "plumbing," dig out all of the crud and open up your spiritual pipes. Most people resent that.

As for me, I would rather endure the chastening of the Lord if He will in turn manifest His glory.

> Ye have not yet resisted unto blood, striving against sin. And ye have forgotten the exhortation which speaketh unto you as unto children, My son, despise not thou the chastening of the Lord, nor faint when thou art rebuked of him: For whom the Lord loveth he chasteneth, and scourgeth every son whom he receiveth. If ye endure chastening, God dealeth with you as with sons; for what son is he whom the father chasteneth not? But if ye be without chastisement, whereof all are partakers, then are ye bastards, and not sons. Furthermore we have had fathers of our flesh which corrected us, and we gave them reverence: shall we not much rather be in subjection unto the Father of spirits, and live? For they verily for a few days chastened us after their own pleasure; but he for our profit, that we might be partakers of his holiness. Now no chastening for the present seemeth to be joyous, but grievous: nevertheless afterward it yieldeth the peaceable fruit of righteousness unto them which are exercised thereby.
>
> **Hebrews 12:4-11**

Chastisement means to inflict punishment on to improve; to discipline or temper; to restrain from excessive or crude behavior. As the Body of Christ, we must elect to endure His chastisement so that it may yield in us the **peaceable fruit of righteousness** (v. 11).

Correction means putting you back on the right course, but *chastisement* means punishment. We don't want to believe that the Lord Jesus punishes His children to correct them. Unfortunately, the definition of chastisement forces us to acknowledge this truth. If He is not correcting and chastening you, the Bible says you are illegitimate and not a true child of God. (Hebrews 12:8; Revelation 3:19.) All of this is a part of studying what His Word really says and not making it say what fits our theology or philosophy concerning it. God will not break your will or spirit, but He will chasten lovingly whom He loves.

Ask yourself, "When you were a child, was not some of the correction you endured actually tough, loving punishment? Are you not the same with your children?" If you answered honestly, why is it so difficult to understand or believe that a holy, loving Father would not chasten you, His child, whom He adores and for whom His Son died?

Furthermore, Jesus suffered chastisement willingly from His persecutors in order to save you completely — mind, body and spirit. (Isaiah 53:5.) This adds a sober, somber note to the truth concerning walking in His footsteps to fulfill our divine commission. But He promised never to leave you or forsake you, even unto the end of the world. (Hebrews 13:5; Matthew 28:20.) On the strength of this truth, we can endure hardness as good soldiers (2 Timothy 2:3), fully understanding what it means to be more than a conqueror through Him Who loves us. (Romans 8:37.) Nothing can separate us from His love. Faith in Him, not in ourselves, causes us to triumph in all things.

Let the Lord Do What He Needs To Do

An awareness of your divine commission means you know that you need correction and that you put away from you the ungodly things shown you about yourself by the Holy Spirit.

That also means putting away all slander, gossip and evil speaking from your mouth. You must respect the persons who are around you in the Body of Christ.

One day, my youngest children at ages three and four were at the kitchen table having an argument. My daughter agitated my son by calling him a "baby head."

Finally, my son replied to his sister, "You, you, you... baby head with a diaper!"

I was at a church not long after that and heard two saints really going at it in the hallway.

Someone asked, "What's wrong with Sister so-and-so?"

I said, "I think someone just called her a 'baby head with a diaper.'"

We need to refrain from that kind of foolishness. God wants to do great things, but we are still caught up in petty judgments and grievances. I mention this because there are still some "baby heads with diapers" out there manifesting in God's Church.

In addition to not slandering the saints, you certainly cannot afford to slander authorities in God's house. People who attend church think nothing of speaking against the pastor or elders and then wonder why their week goes the way it does. They seldom connect what they said about authorities to things not going well in their lives.

They are perplexed when their prayers are like hitting brass in the heavenlies. If you are void of understanding anything involving the church, take it to God in prayerful discussion, not to everyone else. And especially do not slander His generals.

Let us put aside these ridiculous things that divide us, and realize that God has called us to unity like never before in the Body of Christ.

You might say to someone, "I disagree with what you said, but I will stand with you and for you, because you are a man or woman of God." This is the only attitude that will cause us to unify against the true enemy. Unity begets strength and fuels the fire of purpose and goal.

The Tower of Babel was nearly accomplished by people in one accord. (Genesis 11.) How much more so can we accomplish great things if we are unified in Christ?

Do you think all of those "Babel-onians" liked each other? Of course not! But the Bible did not deal with their likes or dislikes of one another. It pointed to their unified efforts and dogged determination that brought God Himself down to investigate their doings.

I hope you are doing such phenomenal exploits in your life that God Himself comes in to investigate. The sad truth is that most of us can't seem to agree with the building committee upon how the natural structure should be constructed. This prevents God from trusting us with constructing the spiritual building. When we finally allow the two foundation stones — the apostle and prophet — along with God's other agents, to rise and orchestrate the spiritual structure, God will firmly establish His Kingdom order, making the Church the most powerful, viable and yes, undefeatable force in the earth. Hallelujah!

Be Who God Called You To Be

One who is aware of his or her divine commission will not try to be exactly like anyone else. Imitation is called the highest form of flattery, but emulation is a sin. (Galatians 5:20.) *Emulation* means to imitate in order to equal or excel; to rival or envy. Emulating causes one to try to become the one toward whom it is focused, denying ourselves the ability to be whom God created us to be. This says to the Father, "You did not create me as good as another," insulting the Father's right to construct divinely each creature.

Some people say things to a child such as, "I wish you were more like your brother or sister."

What a terrible indictment to place upon a child! Let them be unique and discourage emulation. God reinforces our strengths by making Himself perfect in our weakness. (2 Corinthians 12:9.) On the other hand, it should make you proud when you see your children praying as you pray, imitating you as you imitate Jesus, just as the Apostle Paul espouses. To do so means we must truly see Him as He is.

It took a catastrophic event in the Prophet Isaiah's life, the death of King Uzziah of Judah, to cause him to finally see God as He really is and himself through God's eyes. (Isaiah 6:1-13.)

Isaiah's prophecies eloquently fill five chapters before the time when he saw God "high and lifted up." All of what he said was right and true. However, he prophesied without a full understanding of the God whom he was serving and of his own righteousness.

You can be involved in ministry for years and not have a face-to-face encounter with Him. But if you do not have such an encounter, you will never come to greatness. How do you get one? You ask for it. You seek it. You get on your face for it and submit to it. Whatever you need to do, you do it, because you must see Him.

I am unaware of a single true apostle, prophet, or disciple of Christ who did not have a face-to-face encounter with Him and did anything great for Him. In the day you have that divine encounter, your life changes forever. No one will ever be able to turn you aside from the love that you have for Him.

I have been married nearly thirteen years, but I have a new love. I found Him when I was in the middle of great tribulation, turmoil and struggle, often in the midst of ministry. He was there when it felt as though everything would fall apart. He was there to comfort and console, with the fact that with Him everything was going to be all right.

You can become great only if you find the same love that I have found. Is He your everything? Do you know Him intimately? Have you become so incredibly "lovesick" for Him that you push aside your plate, delighting yourself in the food of His nourishing, all-encompassing love?

When life's trials oppress you and the hour appears dark and far spent, remind yourself that in darkness you were created, shaped and knit together, every minuscule part of you. (Psalm 139:11-16.) This revelation will cause you to see that the evening and the morning comprised the first day. God works in darkness as well as in light. You're about to come to the dawning of a new and brighter day.

Everyone impacts someone else's life in one manner or another. How are you impacting those around you or those to whom you are sent? When they imitate you, what are they really imitating? Will the reflection show Jesus, Satan, or fleshly ambivalence through their imitation?

Begin to allow the Holy Spirit to develop these five tenets of greatness in your life in order to serve the Kingdom of God to the best of your ability. Imitate Christ to perfection and discover the full portent of the Great Commission through our Great Commissioner.

Part Two
Don't Let Leprosy Steal Your Legacy

by Mark Chironna

6

From the Call to the Commission

The field of our perception is shaped by the community we are raised in. For most of us, the dominant culture of society is the power that shapes our memories and our hopes. It is also the dominant culture that shapes our beliefs and lends itself to the development or lack thereof of our strengths and weaknesses.

The prophetic vessel is called out of the dominant culture to evoke an awareness of a coming culture, a future culture that embodies the full dream and intention of God in Christ. That culture is a Kingdom culture, where all things are possible. Divine order is present, the power of an endless life is continually being manifested and abundance is everywhere.

Prophets, by their very calling and nature, are visionaries. They are "seers." They "see" the future and call us to live towards that end and live in that end before it arrives. The fullness of Christ and the wrapping up of all things in Christ becomes the consuming passion of these visionaries. Prophets are consumed with a passion for the glory of God and are always concerned about His reputation in the earth.

Moses, in many ways, is the "paradigm prophet" in the Scripture. He plainly states in Deuteronomy 18:15 NIV, **The Lord your God will raise up for you a prophet like me from among your own brothers....** This we know pointed to Christ, and yet the principle we need to remember in dealing with the New Covenant is that what is true of Christ is true of the Church. The Church has become God's prophetic instrument in the world to demonstrate the future in the now.

In that context, God is still raising up apostles and prophets, although some of our brethren in the larger Body of Christ resist that notion. Thankfully, God is not limited to the narrow-minded thinking of systematic theologies that are full of the opinions of men and void of the mind of God. We have yet to see the full disclosure of the power of prophetic ministry in the Church. We are perhaps even now on the verge of seeing a new expression of its genuine restoration in the day in which we are living.

Therefore, it behooves us to pay attention to the examples left us in the Scripture as to the preparation and the pitfalls associated with the vessel God apprehends for prophetic ministry. Since Moses, the great emancipator and liberator of the nation of Israel, is a shining prototype of the ministry of the Lord Jesus, Who made a way for us out of no way, even as Moses worked an exodus event to get Israel out of their affliction, we ought to learn from his humanity the challenges of the call and the commission, lest we repeat the lessons God allowed him to endure. We can learn from his mistakes. (1 Corinthians 10:6.)

The call came to Moses even before he was old enough to be conscious of it. His mother did not fear the edict of Pharaoh, and built an ark to spare his life and sent him down the river Nile, only to be found by Pharaoh's daughter and be spared in the house of the very one who had decreed that he should not live to see his first birthday. He was, by the hand of God, protected and hidden for the purpose of preservation. His mother was paid by Pharaoh's daughter to wean him, and he was raised as Pharaoh's son. The irony of it all is an indication of the wisdom and the power of the Almighty.

Having been weaned by his mother, he was nourished on the milk of an Israelite history. His history and life were bound up with the God of Abraham. The dominant culture of his day, however, was the Egyptian culture, and he was raised in an Egyptian house, under Egyptian rule, with an Egyptian family.

The conflict raged in his young life as the Scripture reveals that at the time of his maturing into his own identity (which psychologists refer to as "self-actualization"), he refused to be called the son of Pharaoh's daughter. (Hebrews 11:24.)

At a significant moment in time, he grappled with the innate sense of the "call" to deliver the people. We know from the Scriptures that the call predates our earthly existence. Paul tells us in Romans 8:30 that those whom He predestined, these he also called.

Somewhere deep in the heart of Moses was the awareness of his destiny. His calling was sure. He was to deliver his brothers. He was "one of them." The challenge, after he slew the Egyptian (Exodus 2:11,12), was to realize that his brothers did not see him as their deliverer. In actual fact, they resented him. Though he was an Israelite by birth, he was raised in the abundance of Pharaoh's house, while they were nourished in the furnace of affliction in the brickyard. They didn't see him as "one of them."

Moses, though acting on his call, was attempting to slay a part of himself when he killed the Egyptian. His bare hands had the kind of strength to take a life. His hands had the energy of years of struggle and pain flowing through them, and the frustration gave vent to the power to take a life in the process.

Moses fled from Egypt because he could not face himself. It was not fear of Pharaoh that made him run (Hebrews 11:27), but the refusal of his brethren to receive him as a deliverer. (Exodus 2:14.) They could not receive someone, though Israelite by birth, who was nourished by the dominant culture. His frustration only intensified.

Forty years on the burning sands of the Sinai deadened the pain, but could not heal it. Dead Egyptians lie under the sand of one whose feet traverse the empty wasteland of unfulfilled hopes and shattered dreams. This one who was called and nourished by the milk of Israel, yet raised by the power of Pharaoh, had a call that would not let him rest, and a people who would not let him lead. The discrepancy drove him further and further into the desert places.

Finally, at the end of a long period of transition, he is apprehended by an uncommon vision. He saw uncommon glory on a common bramble. His view of the future was now being restructured, and his call was about to be ratified by a commission. In the common desert thornbush, as dry as the arid sand itself, burned a flame of passion as intense as the sun. His own life would be characterized by the fiery passion of a vision of God's all-consuming glory, contained in a common, ordinary, dry bramble. The place he had been brought to, and where his feet now stood, was holy. There were no dead Egyptians under that sand. There was no need for sandals to protect his feet from feeling the uneven places on his journey, for he was now on ground that was set apart.

It was here that the commissioning took place. It was here that three signs were given to ratify his calling. It was here where Moses, the visionary, was to be empowered to return to Egypt and impart a view of the future that burned as brightly as the fire in the bramble.

Three Signs of Moses' Commission

The first sign was tied to what he carried naturally in his life for the past forty years. There are things prophetic types carry in their journey that are born out of the process of having to survive with a vision that isn't always readily received.

The staff is a dead thing we lean on when living things give us no comfort. It is something that has been cut off, through which life no longer flows. For Moses and for the people, this is a significant sign. While Moses had indeed killed the Egyptian and buried him in the sand, he could not conceal the pain of his being raised in one culture while being born of another. The dead thing in his hand was the "Egyptian" part of him he could not seem to let go of. It would do us well to realize that he even resembled an Egyptian when he was fully grown, though he was a Hebrew.

The daughters of Jethro took him to be one clearly enough according to Scripture. (Exodus 2:19.) He could not let go of that "dead" thing in his life. It haunted and troubled him for the entire forty years. Only in the presence of glory does he "throw it down." It must be cast down and seen in the light of truth for it to become something living. In actual fact, though the stick was dead, what it really represented in Moses' life was something very alive and even frightening. The snake was merely the manifestation of a part of his life he wished he could forget. He "ran" from what the dead stick became. But snakes can represent more than evil in the life of a visionary.

In order to be effective, prophets must learn how to handle snakes. The prophet, to be an effective voice for the future, must live in a conscious awareness of the hidden and living meaning behind apparently dead things. Moses can't do anything about that of which he is unaware. He must become aware of what is in the stick so that in a moment of time it won't reach out and bite him. He must see things as they really are and not as he pretends them to be. Moses must become whole.

Visionaries, to be truly effective, must be whole. Being whole often means reconciling the opposites in our life that seemingly cancel out our hopes for the future. For Moses, the opposites were the Israelite part of him and the Egyptian part of him. The "serpentine" part of his life had to be integrated into the rest of his life so he could work miracles for others who needed to become whole. It seems as though Jesus was alluding to that when He said, [Be] **wise as** *serpents,* **and harmless as** *doves* (Matthew 10:16).

The *di-vision* in Moses' life needed to become *one vision!* He needed the *wisdom* of his Egyptian upbringing to help him deliver his brethren. Wisdom often appears in forms that frighten us, until we learn to trust God and grasp the hidden wisdom, which is a type of Christ and His ability to rule and transform it for the purpose of ministry. Once transformed, it is no longer a dead staff but a living rod, able to lead a people into the future. The staff served to remind him of his past; the rod served to reveal to him his future. Again, we see the integration of our yesterdays and our tomorrows.

It was King David who said it so well: *...***thy rod** [destiny] **and thy staff** [history] **they comfort me** (Psalm

23:4). My past and my future meet in my present moment, and converge in a dead stick that awaits to be thrown down to show us what lives inside it. When we see the thing in our hand for what it really is, we can be comforted and reassured that our calling is not in vain. It becomes wisdom to us if we grasp it by its tail, trusting God to transform both the stick and our lives in the process.

The intent of the third sign, turning water from the Nile into blood, in some ways implies the significance of war and destruction. The powers of Egypt, manifested in the worship of the Nile, which indeed flowed from one of the four rivers out of Eden, and in the mind of God prior to the fall represented the best of human perception, now represents the worship of the senses to the exclusion of the unseen.

Sense worship denies faith its rightful place. In that regard, Egypt will be destroyed as a reliable place to put one's trust if they want a secure future. The water becoming blood would be a sign of destruction to Egypt, but a sign of victory to Israel. Even as the water and the blood flowed together at Golgotha, what appeared to be defeat was in actual fact victory for the Church. (John 19:34.)

Yet it was the second sign that for prophetic individuals has perhaps the greater significance. Its presence is for our learning and for our legacy. Both the first sign and the second sign are tied to what a hand can grasp. The second sign has to do with what a hand can impart and what a hand reveals. In the second sign, Moses is given clear instruction to lead his hand into the fold of his garment close to his bosom. (Exodus 4:6.) Israel was to emerge as an emancipated nation by the "hand" of Moses. This is the radical nature of his commission.

Prophetically, our hands are guided by our vision. Seventy members of a family entered Egypt to survive while Joseph reigned there with Pharaoh. Four million will leave as a mighty nation under the "hand" of a visionary who tells them that there is life beyond the brickyard, and he will show them where that life can be found. His "hand" will guide them there. That is why the second sign is so vital.

Moses is the first person recorded in all of the Bible as having *leprosy*. Leprosy was the most destructive illness known to humanity in Moses' day. Both Egyptians and Israelites feared leprosy, each for different reasons. The Egyptians saw it as loathsome, and the Israelites saw it as a judgment from God.

When the Scripture tells us that he was instructed to place his hand in his "bosom," it actually means to be "enfolded" in his garment near his bosom. His garment, which is his mantle, is now wrapped around his hand, and his hand is over his heart. When he is instructed to bring his hand out (lead it out), in like manner to how he will lead Israel out from being "enfolded" in the dominant culture of Egypt, he discovers that his hand is leprous.

There was something in Moses' life and in his perception of himself that was diseased. If he is to lead the people out and heal them of their diseases, he must first realize the leprosy that clings to him so readily, and after forty years, is now being revealed.

God's method of deliverance is altogether different than our method. To see the purpose of God is important, to reveal the hand of God in fulfilling the purpose, the way God intends for that hand to be revealed, is absolutely essential.

What Moses saw for his brethren in Egypt was valid because he had accurately discerned God's vision for Israel. What Moses did with his hand when he slew the Egyptian was not valid, because God never intended for Moses to take matters into his "own hand." It was the anger of Moses, and not the glory of God, that was acting in him on that fateful day in the brickyard forty years prior.

It was that crisis that precipitated the long journey into the desert place. It was his "hand" that placed him in the desert to wander as a nomad. It was his "hand" that his brethren were afraid of after they saw him kill the Egyptian. Two of them were fighting on the following day. (Exodus 2:14.) When he endeavored to pull them apart, it was his "hand" they were afraid of. He was asked a pointed question: "Do you intend to kill me, in the same manner you did the Egyptian?" The hand of Moses was what they feared. The hand they needed to trust was leprous. They feared the very hand that was intended to set them free.

Moses needed to learn how leprosy could destroy his future. One could see clearly enough the vision of God, but if one does not allow the heart to be seasoned by grace, the hand will express the frustration that lodges there, and destruction is sure to follow. Moses must look long and hard at his hand in the light of holy fire. Here in God's presence, he must see that his hand is capable of contracting leprosy, if his heart is not seasoned to the point where he learns not to yield to frustration.

Moses is then instructed to place his hand once again into the fold of his robe, near his heart, and then bring it out again. In the second act, his hand is restored. The promise of restoration is something prophets are called to proclaim. The restoration of God's glory in the

earth and of His people is the great cry of the prophets
of old. If Moses will learn this principle, he will not only
be healed of his own leprosy, he will cleanse the entire
Israelite nation by his one "hand," from the defilement
of Egypt.

There are two great prophetic streams of truth that
flow from the river of God in Scripture. The one has to
do with the outpouring of the Holy Spirit on all flesh,
and the other is the restoration of the glory of the Lord
worldwide. Whatever else prophets proclaim, their
voice is a voice of restoration, and their hands are a
demonstration of God's restoring power.

A *leprous hand* is a *frustrated hand*. A *frustrated hand*
is a *hindered hand*. A *hindered hand* is an *unrestored hand*.
One cannot give what one does not have. One cannot
invoke what one does not evoke.

As you look carefully at the life of Moses, it becomes clear that this sign was not heeded fully by Moses.
The same hand that killed the Egyptian became leprous
at Sinai as a sign. It was restored as a promise of hope
for the future. The great tragedy was that the very people
who rejected him the first time he tried to deliver them,
while yet living under Pharaoh's roof, would later
reject him, while under the canopy of the Shekinah in
the wilderness.

You will recall that while Moses went up to the
mountain the first time to see the pattern of heaven, and
to also rebuild it in the earth, he was given two stone
tablets upon which the very finger of God had written
His commandments. While on the mountaintop, it was
revealed to him that the people had fallen into idol
worship. Upon his descent from the mountain, his
anger grew so that when he saw the people worshipping a golden calf, a replica of the Egyptian bull which

represented the god of creation, he smashed the two stone tablets with his *hands*. (Exodus 32:19.)

Upon his descent, the idolatry of the nation filled his vision, and he lost sight of what he saw on the mountain. His hand interfered with God. The difference between what Moses saw on the top of the mountain and what he saw on the bottom of the mountain was a great discrepancy. The discrepancy between what he clearly "saw" as God's ultimate intention and what he "saw" as the current reality of Israel (idolatry), touched off the pain of frustration within him, and his hand destroyed the stone tablets. Then he destroyed the replica of Apis, the bull god of Egypt. The same hand that ground the bull into powder, mixed it with water and made the people drink it.

We might assume that what Moses did was fully acceptable in the sight of God, as many Bible scholars want us to believe. Yet if we follow the trail of Moses' hand over the course of his life, we may, in the end, see a much larger picture of a pitfall that prophets need to avoid.

Frustration is an occupational hazard in the prophetic dimension of ministry. God's servants can be given a clear vision of the end to which God wills to bring His people. The Spirit of the Lord can show it so clearly that there is no question as to the validity of what one has seen. But where God intends to take His Church, and where they currently are, often reveals a gulf so wide that to span it would take decades of the dealings of God, even centuries, or maybe even millennia.

There is a desperate need for vision in the Church. There is a deep cry for the prophetic word in the hearts of the people. The day in which we live is a day of desperation. We need a word from the Lord and we need an open vision.

Acts 23:19ff. tell us that the prophets of old spoke of many things to be restored that the Church still has not seen. They were serving generations yet to be born, while living in a time when what they saw in the lives of the people of God was far from His desired intention. Certainly the pain of carrying the prophetic burden is the frustration of seeing where God intends us to be, and at the same time seeing where the people have a tendency to be. The frustration, if not dealt with, can have an effect on the servant's ability to lead the people.

The possibility of letting the frustration be turned inward (against oneself) or outward (against the people) causes the hand to be susceptible to leprosy. The only proper response is to turn the frustration upward (Godward) and find in Him the power to be transformed by the frustration into a vessel of grace and mercy.

Moses was a prisoner of the letter of the law, and his hand became the only way he saw to adjudicate his frustration. While there were indeed seasons when he "handled" himself in a manner that was beyond reproach, there were those times where his anger overwhelmed him, and the frustration would cling to him like leprosy.

Idolatry is serious business to God, and it hasn't changed much since the beginning. The root of idolatry is really second-hand living. It is an assumption that someone else or something else, other than the living God, has a better way of approaching life and fulfilling it than we have. It is a life lived without taking responsibility for our actions, because we passively are "victims" of the idols of our dysfunctional age. Idolatry parades as worship of God, using the same rituals and routines, but in actuality, it honors the image of something created.

The pathway of depravity in Romans 1 clearly reveals that idolatry is the root of it all. To dishonor God is to exchange the image of glory for a lesser image, perhaps even one of the creations that God made, and then worship it in order to justify behaving like that image.

For Israel to worship Apis the bull is to justify wanting a creative life force that enables us to worship our senses, while we give each other the impression that we are servants of Jehovah.

We live in a day when idolatry parades as the worship of God. Gender confusion and sexual sins have become so rampant in the Church, we now have no sense of conscience about paying to be entertained in the music arena, by individuals practicing an ungodly lifestyle, while singing and preaching in the name of the Lord.

Drugs, immorality and impurity have run their course through the Church world, and we paid for it to keep going on. If someone sings really well, and says all the right words, but has not dealt with the false image they have become, we tend to overlook the transgression and allow that spirit to defile many. We parade our sins openly and place that image on billboards and record labels and market them worldwide.

For the prophetic servant, it is enough to create great frustration. It is far from the intention of God. Yet the anger of man will not achieve the righteousness of God. A hand moved in anger instead of in tempered discipline will fail to cleanse the temple of God from thieves and robbers. Jesus was angered by the idolatry in the temple, but He went out from the temple and

...made a scourge of small cords... (John 2:15). Scholars tell us that to make a scourge of cords from heavy rope-like plants could take hours. What Jesus was doing, in the process of seeing the discrepancy between His Father's vision for His house and the idolatrous state it had fallen into, was to first process His frustration so that His anger was under His control. His hand had to reflect the zeal of the Lord and not the anger of frustration. Indeed, once He made the scourge with His hands, He used the scourge as an instrument in His hand to cleanse the temple. In the process, the authority of God was revealed and the judgment of God was executed, yet the hand of Jesus merely held the instrument of judgment, rather than being the instrument of judgment.

It was the scourge which Jesus made that served the purpose of God to bring the desired result. It was the rod of Moses that God would use in his hand to accomplish his work. It is the rod that is used for correction, not the hand that holds the rod. It is the word of the Lord that brings correction, not the frustrated hand of the visionary that will accomplish deliverance from idolatry.

There are things which need to be addressed in the day in which we live that fall short of God's intention. The challenge for the prophetic ministry is to exercise itself in such a manner as to keep its hands free from the leprosy of frustration.

Thirty-eight years after the incident of the gold calf, the people have still not changed. There came a moment when their thirst became so great that their anger and rebellion once again began to manifest. Moses was given clear instruction from the Lord to gather them at the *rock* which had followed them through the wilderness and to stand by the rock and speak to the rock so that it would bring forth the water. (Numbers

20:8.) The *rock* will yield water of itself. This is the *rock* that Moses had already *struck* once under the command of Jehovah with the rod, and it brought forth water.

We know that the *rock* is Christ and that He was smitten *once and for all* for our failure to live up to the ultimate intention of God. It was necessary for the rod to smite the *rock* the first time. Once the *rock* was split open, water came gushing out. When the spear lanced the side of Jesus, water and blood flowed. (John 19:34.) He has since become the very Source of the river of the water of life. (Revelation 22.) He was wounded *once and for all*. There is no need to strike the *rock* twice, for the fountain is already opened. All that is necessary to satisfy the thirst of the people, even if they rebel, is to speak to the *rock*, and it will release the *water of transformation*.

Moses took matters into his own "hand" for the last time. In Numbers 20:10 he assumes that he must bring forth the water and even says so. He then rebukes the people for their rebellion and takes the rod and strikes out at the *rock* in anger. Scripture says he "smote" the *rock*. (Numbers 20:11.) The word for *smote* is the same word in the original language to describe what Moses did to the Egyptian (Exodus 2:12) and to the tablets and the calf (Exodus 32:19,20), and to the people he commanded the Levites to destroy. (Exodus 32:27.)

The progression, however, is fully manifest. That leprous frustration had fully matured and now "smote" God. The same hand that struck the Egyptian in his youth and struck the people in his middle years now struck the Lord in his latter years. His soul was never fully restored. His hand was never fully freed.

God's verdict for Moses was and is the challenge for all of us who bear the burden of prophetic motivation. The Lord said that Moses would see the land but he would not enter into it. (Deuteronomy 34:4.) The greatest tragedy to occur for those with prophetic vision would be to see where God wants to take them, but never be allowed to enter themselves.

I pray that in these days our hearts and our hands will be fully processed in the presence of His glory so that we can enter into what the Lord is showing us. The good news for us is, there is help and hope available in the New Covenant that can make prophetic ministry so effective and powerful that the Spirit of the Lord can write the vision on our hearts and transform us from within. Then when we place our hands in our bosom, they will come out in the image of glory, restored to their full potential.

For Moses the leprosy was indeed removed. It did not come when he expected it. But generations later, another prophet arose who was called to lead a people out of the bondage of sin into the glorious liberty of the sons of God. At the moment when He needed to prepare for the exodus event (Luke 9:30,31), He went to the top of the mountain and there stood Moses and Elijah. They were sent into the promised land to prepare Him for the exodus He was about to accomplish.

Why would God send Moses to encourage Jesus? When the greatest sign of faith was about to be fought, who better to encourage the Son of God than one who, at the last hour, failed to fulfill his destiny? His failure became the great lesson learned so that the Son of God would not strike back when He was despised and sentenced to death.

There at the Mount of Transfiguration, God turned Moses' failure for good. There he was appointed to encourage the Son of God to trust His Father implicitly and not strike back at the people, but rather to endure to the end and offer the forgiveness that would change the world forever.

May God Almighty raise up true prophetic voices in the day in which we live, who have the power to transform the Church and the world by their words and whose hands are free from the frustration of a leprosy that interferes with the great process of restoration that is taking place in the move of God even as we live!

Part Three
A More Excellent Ministry

by Raphael Green

7

Crafting Witchcraft, Not Shaping Worshippers

Two years ago, I was flying home from a conference when, like a breath, the presence of the Lord came upon me. In the breath were only two words (or messages).

I thought at first everyone heard it, because it sounded like a whisper in the breath of God, "I am grieved."

As I sat there on the plane, I said in my heart, "Lord, about what?"

His response to me was very, very interesting, "I am grieved with My leaders." I said, "Why? and again, in another breath, the word was, "You have crafted witches rather than shaped worshippers."

Witchcraft is not something often associated with the Church, although the Apostle Paul tells us in Galatians 5 that it is one of the manifestations of the flesh. Witchcraft, in essence, is "the lust for and the use of" (to borrow from an eminent teacher in the Word of the Lord) "knowledge and power or ability to control people and events."

Its manifestations are manipulation, intimidation, and domination in order to usurp power and/or authority. We have used Queen Jezebel of Israel, Ahab's

59

wife and high priestess of Baal, frequently to illustrate someone who operates in witchcraft. (1 Kings 21.)

However, the "spirit of Jezebel," or the demonic spirit that influenced and controlled Jezebel, is not operative only in females. This demonic spirit is a spirit of divination. And it is at work in the Church, in both men and women.

Divination comes from the Greek word, *python*, from which we get the word "python." When you study the nature of a python, you see that it does not simply bite and devour its victim, it wraps itself around the victim and suffocates it through constricting motions. In other words, it squeezes it to death and then it devours the prey.

Paul actually had an encounter with someone operating under this demonic spirit. (Acts 16:16-18.) As he preached in Philippi, a young girl began to follow him around and call out concerning Paul and Silas:

> ...These men are the servants of the most high God, which shew unto us the way of salvation (v. 17).

She did this "for many days," Luke wrote. They were correct words, but instead of creating freedom and liberty, which truth always does, her words were suffocating the apostles. The Greek word translated "divination" in her case was *pulon*, meaning "a doorway or gate." She had "a spirit of divination," which meant that she was a channel for familiar spirits, a door for them into this world.

She was manipulating the crowds through true words to eventually follow her and the wrong spirit. Then that Jezebelic python spirit would have tried to usurp the popularity of the apostles for its own benefit.

The Bible says this girl made "much money" for her owners through her fortunetelling. When Paul had had enough of her operation, he turned and cast that spirit out of her — thereby making her owners mad enough to get him and Silas thrown in jail. (Acts 16:19-24.)

I have learned that we need to be careful to discern what spirits are operating through the prophets that we hear. Also, God can send you a word in a tremendous godly anointing. Yet, when it comes to the interpretation, the accurate meaning may be perverted by divination. Think about it. Jeremiah 23 addresses the fact that there can be a vision of the heart that is not of God. The Bible calls it *divination*. It is actually witchcraft, and the only way it can operate is through manipulation, intimidation, and domination.

Our goal ought to be to get back to what God really said and meant. The will of God is for His people to embrace Him, to know Him, to walk with Him, to understand Him, to make Him known and to move in obedience to what He is desirous of doing. (Jeremiah 9:23,24; Philippians 3:1-15; Ephesians 1.) That is our commission.

What Have We Done With Our Commission?

The Lord has been stirring my spirit for some time concerning the concept of our commissions. The word *commission* is a very simple word that basically means "to go (be sent) or to come with an assigned mission, to be joined with a mission." However, it also means "to be sent with a specific task." That means God has given us specific tasks. This is true both individually and corporately.

Most of the time when we think in terms of the Church being commissioned we think of five passages in the Bible, four in the gospels and the fifth in Acts, where Jesus spoke to the apostles about the mission and future of the Church. (Matthew 28:18-20, Mark 16:15-18, Luke 24:48,49, John 20:21,22, Acts 1:8.) Harmonize those verses, and you will see the divine orders that were given for the Church. These orders are usually called "the Great Commission" or "cultural mandate."

In addition to the corporate commission, God has given commissions to individual members of the Body, which, harmonized or combined, will carry out the overriding one. The Bible says you have been called for this purpose, or here is why you have been called, "since Christ suffered for you, leaving an example for you to follow in His steps." (John 12:26.)

Therefore, a foundational aspect of every Christian's commission is *to follow in the steps of Jesus Christ*. This means we are called to show Jesus Christ to the world.

Beverly LaHaye of Concerned Woman for America informed the nation recently that there are about 40 million children in America eleven years of age and under, many of whom are fatherless, jobless, and Godless. The social prognosticators say we have not seen teen violence yet. About half of this next generation are fatherless either physically or practically. In another few years the older of these 40 million youngsters will be teenagers with no jobs and a lot of idle time on their hands.

Most damaging of all, many of them are Godless. There is no intimate communion and, actually, no understanding of a Supreme Creator. The few people who are in place to model the necessary truths of God before them, and the relationship He called us to have with Him, have in a devastating kind of way disappointed many of them.

I believe God is seeking to really jar our thinking and help us to lift our eyes and see 1996 as a year of judgment on mankind in a real sense — yet, it is also a year of harvest. How do we reconcile these two thrusts?

In essence, what God is really requiring is that we become a people who relate everything that we hear, see and experience to Jesus Christ. Logically then, that means we must know Jesus. If we do not know Jesus, with all that is going on around us, we will not only buy into what is presented to us, we will buy into what we are "conned," or what we "con" ourselves, into believing.

God is not going to bless anything other than what He has actually said nor is He going to bless anything He did not mean. Jesus models for us as a human being what it actually takes to fulfill the ministry that we have been called to in Him.

There will be opposition and struggles. There will be a number of things we will encounter. But the normative pattern must be that, when the opposition comes, we continuously entrust or commit ourselves unto him who judges, who appraises situations, and issues and executes verdicts righteously, or justly. (1 Peter 2:21-25.)

In the Bible there are about four or five different ways the word *righteous* or *righteousness* appears, particularly in the part of Scripture we refer to as the "New Covenant" (the Person, the position, the presence, the principles and the practice).

The Bible speaks so clearly about Jesus Christ the Righteous One. Righteousness has a three-fold effect on us: 1) It refers to the Person, Jesus Christ, 2) It is our position *in* that Person, made possible only by His indwelling presence, and 3) It is the practical lifestyle of those who live in that position in that Person. In this manner mankind fulfills the divinely desired, designed and ordained purpose for His existence.

Second Peter 1:3,4 says:

> **According as his divine power hath given unto us all things that pertain unto life and godliness** (that is His presence and the principles), **through the knowledge of him that hath called us to glory and virtue:**
>
> **Whereby are given unto us exceeding great and precious promises: that by these ye might be partakers of the divine nature** (that is the lifestyle in the Person of Jesus Christ) **having escaped** (that is the position) **the corruption that is in the world through lust.**

Righteousness influences us to care about others. Jesus saw the multitudes fainting and scattered abroad without a shepherd, hurting, oppressed by the government and the devil, and lacking knowledge of what their scriptures really meant. (Jeremiah 23:1; Matthew 9:36.)

The Bible says that Jesus, the Righteous One, was moved with compassion. If we are going to walk in the footsteps of Jesus, we have to get His perspective on what ministry really should be and intentionally get involved.

Take Another Look at Jesus' Ministry

My brother and his wife met at Oral Roberts University in Tulsa, Oklahoma, fell in love, married, and now, along with several other assignments, assist in one of the ministries in our local church that feeds the hungry. At first, we did not have people coming to us in such large numbers. However, some of the other food programs in the area began to close, and today, we have virtually an open door to the homeless and needy in our area.

People began to come in off the streets who do not know the Lord, are not churched, and are not familiar with Christian terminology. They have no idea what righteousness means, or even what church means. So we could not impress them with a lot of religious jargon.

However, testimony after testimony is being given of how the Lord has shown my brother and his wife, along with the other people working in this area of ministry, the very method to touch the lives of these people. They do not talk "religious" talk but meet people where they are in compassion. Their actions speak for Jesus.

Without heavy theology or denominational slanted doctrines, they just tell the simple story of Jesus, and people are being saved and helped. The interesting thing is that people who have not been exposed to years of church and who suddenly find out about God and the Bible have no better sense than to believe it!

Those people can walk in miracles easier than some of us long-time Christians. They and others prayed for one new Christian's baby who was dead for about twenty-five minutes, and the baby was brought back to life. God is really seeking to stretch us spiritually, change our thinking, and shift the way we look at things.

When I was a little boy, after I got saved, God began to visit me in dreams and visions repeatedly. And one has stayed with me all of my life. It would happen repeatedly, for weeks on end. Then it would stop, but later, the Lord would bring it back again. This happened for about four or five years between the ages of seven and eleven or twelve.

I would see myself with a treasure chest full of jewels, and the jewels were shining. And one by one, as I would pick them up, I would get caught up in studying them and looking at them from several different angles. Over the years, the Lord began to show me some of the treasures in His Word that have been deposited in me and how we can get focused on only one way of looking at them.

He is requiring that we shift focus. He is going to help us to look at things from the angles He wants, not our traditions. What has been "common knowledge," or the accepted interpretation, of many of the principles we think we know is going to be challenged in the next few years as we seek to be obedient to what God is saying. This is essential in order for us to allow an accurate expression of Christ through us.

In so doing, I am convinced He will have the true worshippers and disciples of the nations that His heart desires, not falsely deified demigods manipulatively and feverishly working to please our flesh or fulfill the ungodly vision spawned by human reason and emotion.

8

Prophets, Priests, and Kings

God is engaged today in preparing a priestly, prophetic, and princely people to carry out His end-time Commission.

In Hebrews we are told a number of things concerning Jesus Christ. He is the visible expression of the radiance of the glory and the exact representation of the nature of the Godhead. He upholds all things by the Word of His power. (Hebrews 1:3.)

The theme of Hebrews is that Jesus is superior to all that was in the old covenant with Abraham and others. Paul wrote the same things in Colossians 1:15-18, where we see that Christ is superior to the entire cosmos, the entire universe. He is the One Who created it, and He is to have preeminence (first place) in all things.

In Hebrews 3, we see that He is the apostle and the high priest of our confession. This was language commonly used, if not spiritually understood always, by those who were a part of Judaism. When someone talked about priests and priesthoods and rituals and so forth, they understood it.

Here in America, we do not really understand the true meaning of many things concerning the temple and tabernacle and the attending priesthood ritual. But the Bible is filled with much symbolism and powerful truths

that help us to understand our walk even as priests.
Hebrews 5:5,6,8-11 says:

> So also Christ glorified not himself to be made
> an high priest; but he that said unto him, Thou art
> my Son, to day have I begotten thee. As he saith also
> in another place, Thou art a priest for ever after the
> order of Melchisedec. (That is from Psalm 110:4.)

> Though he were a Son, yet learned he obedience
> by the things which he suffered; And being made
> perfect, he became the author of eternal salvation *unto*
> *all them that obey him;* Called of God an high priest
> after the order of Melchisedec. Of whom we have
> many things to say, and hard to be uttered, seeing ye
> are dull of hearing.

What is this writer to the Christian Hebrews scattered abroad talking about? He is referring to the
mediatorial ministry of Jesus Christ — His role, His
function, His responsibilities. The Bible says that you
and I have been called for this purpose: To follow or
walk in the footsteps of Jesus Christ. Thus, Jesus Christ's
life and ministry is our supreme model for life and
ministry as well.

For many people, Jesus Christ is still Aaron. Moses'
brother Aaron represents in most Christians' minds the
role of the high priest. However, Aaron was never to be
viewed as a complete shadow or the only type of Jesus.
It is easy from the Old Testament writings to see that
Jesus fulfills one of the main functions of the Aaronic
high priest; i.e., going into the most holy place, once a
year on the day of atonement.

On that day, the high priest offered the blood of
various animals for himself as well as for the nation of
Israel for one year. God instituted this entire act to show
us Jesus and our relationship in Jesus, according to
Hebrews.

In Exodus, we see this annual recapitulation of the blood covenant instituted. In chapter 24, Moses was called into the mount of the Lord (Horeb, or Sinai). On this mountain, he and some of the elders literally saw what seems to have been the view from the bottom up, or the bottom portion, of the throne of God, which looked like sapphires. (v. 10.)

Ezekiel described it somewhat hundreds of years later when he saw it in Babylon. (Ezekiel 1.) However, the most vivid description is found in the Revelation of Jesus Christ, written down by John the apostle on the isle of Patmos. (e.g., Revelation chapters 4, 5, 21, 22.)

But Moses also saw *into* the heavenly sanctuary, Hebrews 9 tells us. What he saw, God said, is a pattern. (vv. 9,23.) Moses literally saw some supernatural beings and items that God wants duplicated on the earth in spiritual terms. This is really what "vision" is about, and this is what it means in a real sense to be prophetic. Everything seen and heard comes from God and is sought to be carried out in obedience to Him and is expressive of what Christ is saying and doing through His Church.

The Earth Is To Duplicate Heaven

Moses was summoned to the mount of the Lord, not because he "had it all together," but because he was God's choice. He was the prophet/judge to whom God chose to reveal the things described in Hebrews. Although Moses did not fully comprehend, God wants it replicated, or duplicated, in the earth realm. That is partly why Jesus said to pray for "the kingdom to come on earth as it is in heaven." (Matthew 6:10.)

There are some key principles we can learn from this. One is that God is obviously to be the center of our lives. Another is that we are to live our lives in two ways:

1) In communion with God; and 2) In carrying out the commission He has given us. Whenever you separate commission from communion, you run the risk of operating upon the unapproved vision of your own heart.

Moses, although from the Old Covenant period, models for us that which is fulfilled in Jesus Christ. Not only are we to be in communion with the Lord, but we have been seated *with* the Lord. This is a powerful, powerful truth that must be understood for us to walk in victory. (Ephesians chapters 1 and 2.)

However, *and this is extremely important in understanding how to follow Jesus,* Aaron is not the complete pattern or model for Jesus. The robes and rituals of the priesthood are "shadows" of things to come, as are the tabernacle and its furnishings. But Jesus is *not* of the Order of Aaron, the descendant of Levi. Hebrews makes that very, very clear. The priesthood was changed. (Hebrews 7.)

What high priestly pattern did Jesus fulfill? That of a mysterious figure in Abraham's life named *Melchizedek,* king of righteousness. A battle occurred in the Valley of Siddim between several kings of Mesopotamia. Those who won took Abram's nephew Lot, his family, and all his belongings as spoils from Sodom and Gomorrah. (Genesis 14.)

The Bible says that Abram took 318 men of his household trained to fight, and they went and recovered everything from those kings. Bringing back the choicest of the spoil with him, he is met by the "king of righteousness from Salem" (Peace), who appears without genealogy.

Hebrews says he modeled Christ for us. Some Bible teachers even claim that he *was* Christ in an Old

Testament appearance. However, I would say rather that he models Christ for us. He is a shadow of Christ.

A shadow is a "picture" or reflection cast on a wall or background because light shines on a person or thing of real substance. So Melchizedek was a shadow of the real Priest and King, Christ Jesus.

The writer of Hebrews is talking to us about a man who, by God's divine design, has shown us a bit about Who and what the Anointed One would be like. Not a whole lot was written about Melchizedek.

Under the Old Covenant, there was normally the separation of the offices and functions of priests, prophets, and king. However, Melchizedek models for us what God really has in mind as an end result for His people through Christ.

The writer of Hebrews, whom some think was Paul, rebuked those to whom this letter was sent because they had become hard of hearing, no matter how much they had already learned. Those who ought to have been able to explain these truths had lost sight of them for themselves. (Hebrews 5:11-14.)

Explaining is really what a teacher does. It is one of the figurative meanings of the Greek word for "laborer." When Jesus said, "The harvest is ripe, but the *laborers* are few" (Matthew 9:37), the word means "toilers." However, that particular Greek word also was used figuratively for "teachers."

You see, a part of the divine commission that God has given us is that we are to be disciplers of the nations, not just evangelizers. "Go ye therefore and...." The actual Greek word there is, "Make disciples continuously of the nation."

A part of the commission is that every one of us, although we may not be serving governmentally as teachers in the house of the Lord, will function to some degree in the ministry of teaching. It is a "toiling" ministry. Yet, it is very essential to fulfill the Great Commission and operate in the more excellent ministry of Christ.

We Are Also "Dull of Hearing"

This warning about becoming "dull of hearing" is sandwiched in a number of warnings the writer has already given to those who are now considering leaving the faith. They were warned of neglect, of hardness of heart, and of an evil heart of unbelief that can lead to departing from the living God.

There are those who are doubting Christ and, apparently, they are doubting whether or not they have actually believed on the right person. So this writer explains to them under the inspiration of the Holy Spirit who Jesus Christ really is and that he is not of the same order as Aaron. The writer actually pointed out some very key principles they need in order to hold onto what they have learned about Christ.

In other words, if we are going to be effective and do what God calls us to do, we have to go back to understanding Christ after the order of Melchizedek. If we have never heard it, or if we have, but have forgotten it, the Word of the Lord comes to bring us back to a healthy and vital understanding concerning our position of fellowship, communion and commitment in Christ.

If I am hearing from the Lord correctly, there are a number of persons who have "gone off on the deep end" prophetically because they did not know the first principles related to Christ. It is one thing to tell you about cars and houses, or a woman or man coming into your life, but it is another to understand those issues and things in the light of Jesus Christ and His purpose for you personally and corporately.

Remember, Paul did not simply pray that we receive the spirit of revelation and wisdom, he prayed that we would receive the spirit of revelation and wisdom *in the knowledge of Christ.* (Ephesians 1.) So if God is speaking to you about something material, you can rest assured that is not all there is to that prophecy. In it, there is something about the Christ which He wants you to know and allow to be expressed through you.

So much of what is being taught in the Church today is basically milk. There is a place for milk, but we need the meat for the protein. We have to have more. Jesus really understood the order of Melchizedek. And this understanding was directly connected to the maturity and perfection of His ministry.

It is a first principle in a real sense. Some people call those verses in Hebrews 5 "a transitional message." Yet, notice how it feeds into the traditional first principles that most of us know about in Hebrews 6:1,2. For everyone who partakes only of milk is not accustomed to the word of righteousness or the message of righteousness. Not every Christian understands the priesthood of Jesus in light of the righteousness He gives. That is part of the reason nothing much is happening.

If every Christian in America won one Christian, in two or three years our nation would be covered. That is "exponential" growth. If we would each win one this year and disciple each soul to win another one next year, it would be over.

But what is the problem? We have crafted witches, rather than shaped worshippers. We are in it for us, not for righteousness. Solid food is for the mature, who through practice have their senses trained to discern good from evil, God from Satan, the noble from the ignoble, and righteousness from unrighteousness.

Discernment is something that comes as you practice or exercise it. The ability to actually judge with critical God-given analysis what is going on in a situation requires that you step into it to even begin to move in discernment.

God in essence is calling us to a mature understanding of our Commissioner and commissions. The unity God is dealing with us about is not a unity of spirit only, which we already have through the Holy Spirit, whether we honor that or not. (Ephesians 4.) The call to "unity" today has to do with *unity of understanding.*

Pressing on to Maturity

This is going to require some effort on our parts individually to respond to what God is saying to us, not just the effort of the ministry of the spoken Word or of the one ministering the Word. Sometimes I think that, with all of the good teaching in the past two decades, we have information overload.

Also, there have been some oversimplification and some "scaling down" in our interpretations of the process God will allow us to go through to be prepared for and fulfill His purposes. If we are going to do what God has called us to do, we are going to have to put forth some effort.

Obedience involves much more than the acquisition of things. The ministry of Jesus Christ through us, as when He was on earth, is one of maturity, one of excellence.

In Philippians 1, Paul prayed for the Church to come into a full knowledge of the love of Christ and be able to discern that love. Why? In order that we may approve the things that are *excellent* and give the fullest expression of what God is about. Life in the most holy place is where you and I are. (Hebrews 6; Ephesians 1,2.)

Ephesians 2 says that God *made us alive in Christ, raised us up together in Christ,* and *seated us together in Christ.* Where is Christ?

Unlike Aaron, Jesus did not simply go in, offer His blood in the most holy place in the heavenly sanctuary, and come out. He put His blood on the altar only once for all sin (past, present, and future). Then He took a seat at the Father's right hand. And Scripture says you and I have been raised up and seated together in Christ. The phrase *seated together* means a Kingdom has been conferred on us.

The "more excellent ministry" of Jesus then is not simply grabbing a truth and concentrating or building camp on it. God wants us to press into *Him,* not flounder in the disagreements about basic, biblical foundational truths that we create movements around. God would have us embrace Who Christ is and what His purpose is for these foundational truths.

There are promises in the heart of God that have been released to us relating to what *He* desires to see expressed in the earth. When we begin to embrace those promises according to the way that God means them, we are going to be able to move into that which God desires for us.

I believe there are apostolic, prophetic, pastoral, evangelistic, and teaching ministry giftings that have to take place in other contexts than within the local church. This is part of God's hope. (Ephesians 1.)

Hope in Scripture never means simply an earthly wish or dream. It always means a desire and expectation birthed in us by the Spirit and based on the Word of God. When Paul prayed in Ephesians 1 that followers of Jesus would receive the spirit of revelation and wisdom in the knowledge of Christ, it was for three specific reasons:

1. That we would know the *hope* of His calling; that is, actually experience and live out the desire and the expectation that is in God concerning His Church.

2. That we would know, or experience, the wealth of the riches of His inheritance in the saints. That is the covenant relationship and benefits through His indwelling presence.

3. That the surpassing greatness of His power would become known to those of us who believe in some manner He raised Christ from the dead and seated Him at His right hand. (Ephesians 1:20,21.)

We are to know the desire and expectation that is in the heart of the Father. What is His desire and expectation concerning this nation? What are the riches of His inheritance in the saints? What is the surpassing greatness of His power?

Maturity Must Be for Each of Us

I asked the Lord once, "Why are you not doing some of the things You showed me that You were going to do through me?"

And the Lord spoke to my heart, "Because in your heart there is an unhealthy attachment between your self-esteem and what I promised."

Then He asked, "Why am I not enough?"

And I had to examine myself to see what had me pursuing ministry to fulfill my self-esteem rather than pursuing God.

Another thing He said was, "A man skilled in his labor, in his work, shall not stand before obscure men."

God was saying to me, "You are not ready. You are not as far down the road as you think you are, or as you want to be. You are not doing what you think you are doing."

Much of what God had told me to do was being tainted by my own interpretations. He could not allow that pattern of behavior and erroneous thinking to remain and still release me into the thing He had promised. As I examined my life and motives, I began to see something.

When I was a little boy I used to sit and watch Oral Roberts and Billy Graham preach, and I remember often the presence of God would come upon me. I was ten years old when I sat and watched them preach. God would speak to my heart about ministering His Word one day, and I created an image for myself that was not from God.

So, as an adult minister, when God would lead me in directions that did not look like they were leading toward my "vision," I resisted them. What I thought had come from Him was actually from my own mind, also influenced by doubt and by divination.

If you do not understand that Jesus literally has gone into the heavenlies as our forerunner after the order of Melchizedek, you are not going to understand your commission any better than I did. Most of us relate our commissions to the earthly patterns and

traditional ways of ministry with which we are familiar. So self-esteem, control, and materialism "kick in"
to pervert our goals from God's. We need to stop and
find out what ministry is really all about to Christ.

The writer of Hebrews was saying to all the Jewish
people who had come into Christ, "The priesthood has
been changed! The real thing has arrived which
Melchizedek foreshadowed, and Aaron's order is
passed. It is done away with."

This is not something to do religiously. The
righteousness we received has not been earned by
us but freely imputed, or credited, to us. The right
standing (position) before God which we receive at
conversion is something given (imparted) to us also,
not something we earned. (Ephesians 2:8,9; Titus 3:5;
Romans 5:17,18.)

If we are going to call this next generation to
participate in the righteous nature of Jesus, we are
going to have to deal with them where they really
are. Yet, we must present a ministry and message
of hope that goes way beyond what we do for them
physically.

Jesus once asked a rather scary question, "When
the Son of man returns, will he find faith on the earth —
or, when the Son of man returns, will he find a people
who are hearing, agreeing and obeying according to the
insight of God?" (Luke 18:8.)

Will He find a people who have "seen," heard from
God, agree with God, and obey God?

Will they have been able to traverse, navigate, and
work their way to a place where they are hearing, agreeing, and obeying what God is saying, or will they just
be out there aimlessly floating around?

Will I find a people who not only gather to hear the Word and be inspired, but a people who will be obedient to what I have meant?

Will I find a people I can stretch and turn and use in my own unique way to fulfill what is in My Spirit for this land?

When the Lord began to deal with my heart about these kinds of things, I had to see that a lot of what I was focused on involved visions I had made. What God was really trying to get me to be was not a celebrity, but a servant.

To get in alignment with Him and out of doing my own thing, I had to change some things. I had to be willing to be anonymous. When the Apostle Paul talks about being a faithful *steward* of the revelations God had given him, the actual word means an "underrower." That was someone in the ancient ships who sat on the bottom, along with many other unknown men, rowing to give the ship mobility.

He was saying, "I may not be seen; however, the one thing that is important is not that I be famous, but that I be faithful. I have dreamed sometimes of things that were not my lot, but, oh, the joy of knowing I am doing what I was called to do. The thing that anchors me emotionally and mentally, that even anchors me in my physical body is not what people think of me, it is what Jesus thinks."

The majority of the people who are going to be won to the Lord over the next five years, will not be won in great massive crusades alone, but by people who are definite disciples because they will be not only skilled in the Word of righteousness, but will be mature followers of Jesus who move in "the more excellent ministry" of the ultimate Prophet, Priest, and

King, Christ Jesus, as His priestly, prophetic and princely (kingly/royal) people.

Part Four
Ambassadors of Reconciliation

by David Ireland

9

The Difference Between Grace and Mercy

Recently, I had a dream, and in the dream, I saw an older minister who represented "the old guard" and a younger minister representing "the new guard."

The older minister was totally caught up with fulfilling his ministry and the purpose of God for his life. He never took time to consider for a moment that perhaps part of his calling was to mentor the younger man. And he died not having been a spiritual father to the new guard.

True leaders recognize that there is another generation after them. A leader only becomes effective when he or she realizes they are not going to live forever. When the Apostle Paul realized he was going to die, he began to impart what he knew to others. Jesus mentored, or discipled, others. Moses trained Joshua.

Everyone who understands he is not going to live forever in the physical body recognizes the importance of imparting truths, principles, and information that will help the new guard.

For some time I looked for a spiritual father. I searched high and low. A lot of times I spent time around men who were incapable of mentoring me, either out of jealousy or envy, or they were awkward.

Finally, the Holy Spirit spoke to me and said, "David, stop looking for a father and *be* a father."

In order to mentor others, one must be an "ambassador of reconciliation" between generations, as well as races, classes, genders, and nationalities. One must learn the difference between *grace* and *mercy* as a starting point.

Grace and mercy often are used interchangeably, as if they are synonyms, but they are not. Grace and mercy are distinctly different from one another.

It may help to imagine the heavenly council before the beginning of time and see God standing up at the board meeting saying, "I am a God of justice. I must be able to establish equity, fairness, and judgment. Anyone who sins against Me is worthy of damnation."

You can see His hand as it hits the table. "I am a God of justice!"

Then Mercy cries out, "But God, You also are a God of mercy. How could You be both in the same breath?" Now we see a little dilemma.

Mercy and Justice are going at it, trying to find out how God could be filled with justice and equity, yet at the same time, be merciful. As they are hashing out the issue, perhaps Grace stood up and said, "I have a way for God to be both just and merciful at the same time."

And Scripture says in John 1:17 that there He is — Jesus Christ, full of grace and truth! So we see that one of the greatest aspects of the nature of God and His essence and uniqueness is His grace.

Mercy Pardons, Grace Does Much More

Let us assume you went into a convenience store late at night to rob the place. The surveillance camera caught your picture as you walked over to the clerk and said, "Put your hands up and open the cash register! How much money do you have in there?"

The clerk opens the drawer and says, "I have about $500."

"Give me the $500, and move over to your left."

He moves over to his left, where unbeknownst to you there is a private alarm hooked into a police station. So a squad car full of police catch you in the middle of the act. They usher you off to jail for a speedy trial and bring you before the judge for sentencing.

The judge said, "Sir, do you realize what you have done is a crime?"

"Yes, sir."

"Do you realize I can throw you in prison?"

"Yes, sir."

"Do you realize you are a thief? Do you realize that?"

"Yes, sir."

"Approach the bench. You are a thief, but I am not going to throw you in jail. Today I am going to show you mercy — get out of here. Run as fast as you can, you are pardoned." That is mercy.

Let us change the scenario now, so we can understand grace. In the courtroom, the judge says, "Sir, do you realize what you have done is wrong?"

"Yes, sir."

"Approach the bench. I understand you were trying to steal $500. Here is $500. I understand you do not have a job. I want you to show up here Monday at 9 a.m. You are going be my assistant. I understand you do not have a car. I have a second car that my wife and I do not use. Here are the keys." You have received grace.

Perhaps this example will allow us to understand more specifically what Luke meant in Acts 4:33 when he said that great grace, or abundant grace, was upon every single one of the first Christians in Jerusalem, from children to adulthood. Not only did they receive the grace of God that brought them into salvation, but the manifestation of God's grace upon their lives.

Grace is the English translation of the Greek word, *charis*, which originally meant "great beauty." When the New Testament writers used the word, they were talking about the beautiful favor of God. Grace is more than God's unmerited favor.

In my studies, I ran across another definition which I like better: Grace is the enabling presence of God that empowers me to be what He called me to be and to do what He called me to do.

So Acts 4:33, means that everyone from the oldest to the youngest knew they could fulfill their destiny in God: **And great grace was upon them all.**

From the ones who went into full-time ministry to the ones who did not, from the ones who were just saved to the ones who had walked with Jesus for years, from the ones struggling with different areas of their lives to the overcomers in every area — everyone experienced abundant grace. They received not only grace for salvation but grace for growing in the empowering presence of God.

How do we get grace in our lives? There is a place you can walk that opens your life to receiving grace while being a conduit for God to give grace to others through you.

10

How To Receive and Give Grace

The Bible speaks of several different ways to obtain grace in your life. James wrote that God resists the proud and gives *grace* to the humble. (James 4:6.) Therefore, one of the ways to obtain grace is by *walking in humility*.

Humility is a posture of looking at oneself in a subservient way compared to God. It is bending one's knees before God. It is saying that you are dependent on God, not on self.

A second way in which I can get grace in my life is what Paul told the church at Ephesus: We are saved by grace through *faith*. Faith is the doorknob. When I turn the knob, it opens up to grace. I like to look at faith as an acronym, "Full assurance in the heart, free access into the heavens."

When I am fully assured in my heart and will not be persuaded otherwise that God is going to work that which is in accord with His Word in my life — that is faith. So *faith opens the door to grace*.

A third way of obtaining grace in your life ties into the idea of calling forth the new guard. We understand this principle in other areas of life. It is called *"the law of reciprocity,"* or as it is found in Galatians 6:7, "the law of sowing and reaping."

If I sow grace, I reap grace. What exactly is "sowing grace"? Scripture tells us plainly that you and I can give grace to people, and the way in which we give grace to people is by what comes out of our mouths, and how it is received.

Peter wrote, **But grow in the grace, and in the knowledge of our Lord and Saviour Jesus Christ** (2 Peter 3:18.)

Paul wrote in Ephesians 4:29, **Let no corrupt communication** (no unwholesome word) **proceed out of your mouth, but that which is good to the use of edifying, that it may minister grace unto the hearers.**

Paul also wrote in Colossians 4:6, **Let your speech be alway with grace, seasoned with salt, that ye may know how ye ought to answer every man.**

So we see clearly then from Scripture, you and I are vessels, or conduits, who can dispense the grace of God. The salutation in many of the epistles in the New Testament is, "Grace to you. May you receive God's grace."

In other words, the writer was saying, "I am a conduit of the grace of God. May you be the recipient. May you receive the empowering presence of God in your life that will enable you to be what God created you to be and to do what God called you to do. May you receive that. Grace to you."

When you sow grace, you receive grace. Paul wrote to the church at Corinth that he wanted to let them know that *the grace of God* had been given to the churches of Macedonia. Those churches were into hard times, but in the middle of affliction and poverty, they had experienced joy in donating money out of their need to the saints in famine in Jerusalem.

> ..But first gave their own selves to the Lord, and unto us by the will of God. Insomuch that we desired Titus, that as he had begun, so he would also finish in you [the Corinthians] the same grace also. Therefore, as ye abound in every thing, in faith, and utterance, and knowledge, and in all diligence, and in your love to us, see that ye abound in this grace also.
>
> 2 Corinthians 8:5-7

How did they receive the grace of the Lord Jesus? Grace is received when there is a need. Let us confirm that by 2 Corinthians 9:8:

> And God is able to make all grace abound toward you; that ye, always having all sufficiency in all things, may abound to every good work.

Look for Someone To Help

Most of the time we look for someone to raise us up, someone to help us understand our ministry, someone to help understand and interpret our dreams and visions, our lifelong ambitions.

Rather than asking God to send someone to help you, try saying, "God, send *me*. I want to be a conduit of Your grace. I want to be used by You to help someone unlock their destiny. I want to be used to help someone come into their calling in You."

Many of us go through depression and various emotional changes, because we do not know where we are in God. Or because we have come to some type of impasse in our maturation with God. Remember Elijah? The prophet was suicidal. Why? It was because a woman threatened him. He ran and hid in a cave and went into severe depression.

What does he do in the midst of depression?

The great prophet of God ran into a cave and begged, "God, kill me now!"

He did not want to kill himself, he wanted God to kill him so he could blame God. You would think God would rebuke him. We would rebuke him, because we do not look at things from God's perspective.

We would say, "Look at you! You are supposed to be a great man of God. Come on, where is your backbone? You are a spineless man. You are no real prophet of God!"

Most of us would take a strong confrontational approach to straighten out the prophet. But God does not.

God tells the suicidal, depressed prophet, "Elijah, go raise up Elisha, the son of Shaphan, who is plowing with twelve yoke of oxen. Raise him up to be a prophet to take your place."

The answer to suicide and depression is to begin to impart what you have to someone else. Many times we do not go where we are supposed to in God because of never pouring our lives into someone else.

When you begin to impart to someone less than you in God, it means you have a Kingdom mindset. You are interested in building God's Kingdom, not yours. God is concerned about global missions. God is concerned about what you and I must do to reach the world for Him.

When someone is depressed, they are not reaching out to others. Cutting-edge ministry is reaching someone else. It takes a lot of patience to work with individuals who are immature in God. However, patience really is a form of grace. It takes a whole lot of grace to work with people.

If the Church in America reached out to people who were in need, the Church would double immediately. Every one of us knows people who are in need, not just physical need, but emotional and psychological need. I am talking about the need to communicate, the need for companionship.

Many Christians pray for God to send us to the far-reaching places of the world, but we forget about the people right next door. Husbands and wives forget about each other and about the children and family members.

We cannot hear from God to minister to our wives, because we are trying to hear about ministering to someone in the Sudan, and then we wonder why God does not hear us.

Perhaps the classic account of one showing grace to another and being encouraged to do that is the story of the runaway slave, found in the Apostle Paul's letter to Philemon.

Philemon was a well-to-do Christian who had the local church meeting in his home. One of his slaves had run away and somehow ended up in Rome where he was exposed to Paul's preaching from prison and got saved. Paul sent this slave back to his master with a letter.

Those who get saved then have an obligation to make restitution where needed or to make things right that they have done wrong, if possible.

Two thousand years ago slavery was a custom all over the world, and it did not just affect blacks. Whoever conquered took those conquered and made slaves of them, or at least, some of them. Also, if you could not pay your debts, you ended up as a slave of the one you owed.

Onesimus was a runaway slave, whose "slave name" meant "Useful." That was not his birth name. When a slave was sold, usually he stood on a large platform in the central marketplace stripped naked so potential buyers could see if he or she had any physical defects.

When Philemon bought this youth, or man, he named him what he wanted him to think about and what he wanted him to become. He named him *Useful*; however, the man was useless.

Philemon was trying to do all that God wanted him to do. He was trying to walk in the grace of God. This slave was supposed to help him become a better steward by helping him increase his financial holdings and all his material resources. Instead, this slave even stole from Philemon. Now he is a useless, runaway thief.

For that reason, Paul wrote that, "If he has wronged you in any way or owes you anything, charge it to my account." (v. 18.)

Shame Hinders Destiny

Can you imagine the shame that was over this man's head? Shame does not mean you have done something wrong. Shame means you *are* someone wrong. If you do something wrong and are aware of it, you probably are ashamed, but shame is not part of your personality or your integrity of self.

People who have been abused physically or sexually walk in shame, not because they did something wrong, but because they think something is wrong with them. So the emotion of shame is an awesome and horrible feeling. People filled with shame never can complete their destiny. Dignity impacts destiny.

How I think about myself affects whatever I will do for God. Many times, we do not realize the issue of dignity is impacting the Church. There are many people in Father's house who are walking in shame, who are living under the guilt and the condemnation of shame, living below their dignity in God.

You and I, who have been impacted and empowered by the presence of God, who want to receive the grace of God in our lives, must realize that God has called us to be *ambassadors of reconciliation*, to restore individuals to a place of their potential in God.

Those of us who are searching, probing, striving, lunging, reaching towards heights and depths in God to mature, must remember to reach down to those who are struggling. Reach down to those who are lowly. Reach down to those who are wallowing in shame and in the quagmire of this life. When you do that, you are recognizing what it means to be an authentic reconciler in the Kingdom of God.

Philemon is a short letter; however, if you read it carefully, you will see that it shows Paul in his role of "master builder" of people. He is a master apostle. True apostolic ministry does not "lord it" (exercising authority) over people.

Those whom God has given authority in my life build me up. People who have no authority in my life tear me down. I do not have to be a great mind to figure out who are the authority figures in my life. I simply look at who is building me up and who is tearing me down.

Prophets have the ability to choose words that do not maim those who hear the accurate word from God. The Father is not interested in hurting, the Father is interested in helping. When Nathan was sent to David, he chose his words properly. He knew David's conscience. Although David had fallen into sin, he was still a man of integrity.

So Nathan the prophet presented his prophetic message in a way that reflected integrity in order to reach the heart. Once he got to David's heart, he could get David on his knees in God. Nathan's word from God was presented in terms to cause David to be ashamed of what he had done and repent. Nathan did not, however, heap shame on David to maim his soul.

Parents need to correct what children do in such a way as to bring contrition, not attack the child's personality and build shame into his character. Say, "What you did was wrong" (implying you are okay but your action was not). Do not say, "*You* are no good and will never amount to anything."

A True Mentor Encourages Instead of Judging

Paul was a wise apostle. In that one short letter taking up one page in our Bibles, he used three selling points to bring Philemon to a place where he would operate in grace. You can tell a wise leader by the people around him.

If I see no one behind you, you are not a leader. On the other hand, if I see people cowering behind you, they are scared, which means you are not a biblical leader, but a despot, an Idi Amin. You are not a leader whom God has raised up, or at least you are not operating rightly in His grace.

Paul, in his imprisonment, begot Onesimus in the faith. The Bible does not tell us the circumstances, the way, the reasons, or how it all came about. However, finding Onesimus presented Paul with a legal dilemma, and Paul always upheld the law of the land. He was a Roman citizen.

Roman law said that if you found a runaway slave, you had one option — send him back. If the slave absolutely refused to go, he was to be sold into slavery again wherever he was. The money from the sale then went to the previous owner. If you chose not to do either of those things, you were in trouble along with the slave.

Paul not only had gotten Onesimus born again, Paul was mentoring Onesimus. Mentoring, or discipling, people means bringing them to a certain level of maturity. Once we get them there, the issue becomes an issue of grace.

There are things in people's lives they can never circumvent, never avoid, never erase, never sweep under the rug. They must be dealt with. Although Onesimus was born again, he was still a runaway slave. Although he now had aspirations of ministry and was very helpful to the great Apostle Paul, that did not change his status as a slave.

Paul recognized that his mentoring, his imparting to Onesimus only brought him to a certain spiritual place, because there were issues in Onesimus' life that must be dealt with. The issue was one of shame. The issue was one of his past. The issue was one of guilt. The issue was the fact that he was someone's property, but he had run away.

In order for Onesimus to be what God called him to be, he had to find grace from Philemon — not God, not Paul — Philemon. There are people in our lives who need our grace — not God's grace, not the pastor's grace, our grace.

If we are the ones needing grace, we must understand that we cannot force someone to be gracious to us. I cannot force my wife to love me. I cannot put a gun to her head and say, "Love me or else." I cannot pout and do various manipulative things to get her to love me. She must arrive to a state of love by her own volition. I cannot force it.

In the same way, you cannot force someone to pour out grace to you. You cannot force someone to speak to you in a gracious way. You cannot force someone to dispense grace to you. It must be of their own accord. They must initiate. They must see the need, want to extend grace to you, and then dispense it.

Paul then had to get Philemon to a place where he would freely give grace to Onesimus. The apostle essentially was mentoring both of them, acting as an *ambassador of reconciliation*.

Onesimus could not be what God called him to be unless he received grace from the one to whom he owed much. He needed Philemon's grace when, actually, Philemon could have killed the man right there. He would have been legally safe to do so.

Put yourself in the position of Philemon. You have just lost $10,000 (the going price for a slave like Onesimus), plus perhaps the $10,000 he had stolen and another $10,000 spent searching for him. Here is this man who has the audacity to come back to you in person, after you have sent others to scour the land to find him.

Onesimus stands there, perhaps with his head lowered. He probably was afraid to look his master in the eye, in case he misread the situation. Philemon faces his runaway slave, and perhaps his face begins to contort in anger and his body starts to get rigid.

Onesimus, recognizing the signs, thrusts a piece of parchment into Philemon's hand and says, "From the Apostle Paul."

You straighten up when you hear or see someone who means something to you, so Philemon's countenance begins to change as he reads Paul's word, **Grace to you, and peace, from God our Father and the Lord Jesus Christ** (v. 3.)

The first third of the letter deals with how much Paul thinks of Philemon and what good things he is hearing about him and his ministry to the saints. Then, he points out that he is an old man in prison for the sake of Jesus and asks a favor of Philemon out of love.

Three Ways of Encouraging Others To Show Grace

The first way the master apostle gently pointed out to Philemon the need to show grace was to remind him that he had been a recipient of grace. You cannot be judgmental, harsh, and vindictive when you have been a recipient of grace yourself.

So he pointed out, "Philemon, buddy, you are who you are because you have received the grace of God. How can you now exact judgment and penalties against Onesimus, when you, too, have received grace."

Unfortunately, the easiest and, usually, the quickest response to wrongs for human beings, even Christians, is a response of judgment. It is a response that is harsh. It is a response that says, "Condemn, maim, annihilate."

When you hear that someone has done something horrible, and then God sends you to deal with that person, you know the bad things you can prophesy. Yet, if you are truly hearing God, most of the time grace comes on you in the presence of that person — like Nathan with David!

You had the "hatchet," but now the hatchet has been put away, and you are weeping with the sinner, because the grace of God has been poured out through you.

The second way the master pushed Philemon toward dispensing grace was by communicating to him the idea the same situation might have befallen him but for *the grace of God* dispensed through Paul. (v. 19.) When we understand fully that the old saying, "There but for the grace of God go I," is absolutely true, we are in a place to be able to reach out in grace to others. We are ready to serve them, rather than judge them.

The third point Paul used was to point out that God's goal is to present everyone of us to Himself, spotless and without blemishes. (Jude 24,25.) If God's goal is to present every born-again person to Himself without spot, without blemish, whole before Him, you and I are co-laborers with the Lord. Our job is to help present every person we can faultless and blameless before God.

The master apostle was saying, "Philemon, your goal in life is not to exact punishment against Onesimus. Your goal in life is to help Onesimus be what God has called him to be."

What happened in this case? The Bible does not tell us, although we can assume that Philemon, being as good a follower of Jesus as Paul thought, would have honored Paul's request and pardoned his former slave.

However, Church history may give us the answer. When Ignatious, bishop of Antioch, was being led to Rome to be martyred in A. D. 110, he wrote a letter. In it, he made several references to the bishop of Ephesus.

A bishop historically is a pastor's pastor, an overseer not only to his own parish, but to his geographical area. The name of the bishop of Ephesus, to whom Ignatious referred, was *Onesimus*. Assuming the annals of Church history are correct, it means that the runaway slave and thief, full of shame, guilt, and condemnation, received grace from Philemon.

Onesimus received the empowering presence of God that enabled him to be what God had in mind for him to be and to do what God called him to do. Here was a man who could have been judged, could have been punished, and could have been legally put to death. Years afterwards, he is an overseer of the churches at Ephesus. Why? Because someone showed him grace.

Perhaps God is looking for us to help raise up people, to look for the Onesimuses in our lives, the runaway slaves, the thieves. Look for those who are under shame, those individuals who are so easy to judge. It is so easy to exact justice, to sweep certain people under the rug, to push them away and erase their existence.

There are people in your life who need your grace. They need to hear your words, they need to hear your thoughts, they need to hear your decisions. They need to hear your judgment, they need to hear your opinion, they need to hear what your thoughts are on the matter. What you sow is what you reap.

The best way we can call forth the new guard is by showing grace, by becoming *ambassadors of reconciliation.*

Part Five
Replacing Principalities

by Paula Price

11

Apostle Is a Synonym for Principality

One synonym for apostle is *principality*. We have not understood principalities because of Ephesians 6:12 in which Paul wrote about demonic powers assigned to the earth and their affairs under Satan.

> For we wrestle not against flesh and blood, but against principalities, against powers, against the rulers of the darkness of this world, against spiritual wickedness in high places (or, against spiritual houses in the heavenlies).

Principality simply means someone in authority over a certain territory, which also is called "a principality." It does not mean just demons, although some demons fill the offices of principality. A governor of a state is technically a principality, ruling over certain territory.

We have had a move in the Church for several years of pulling down "principalities" in the heavenlies. If they are removed, who then is going to rule over earth's systems? Instead of evil and darkness, are we to have chaos? Are angels to fill those offices usurped by Satan and his ruling powers?

No, the Bible says the Body of Christ is the authority delegated to rule in the spiritual realms of the earth. It seems those principalities and powers in the heavenlies are like the heathen, ungodly tribes in the Promised Land. They are defeated, yet they have to be run out of the territory. And God would not run them out all at once, lest the land be overrun with weeds, thorns, and thistles.

Principality is "the state of being first or high in rank." It is an office of authority and the power of a prince, the offspring of a king. It is princely dominion. In an earlier chapter Raphael Green wrote about becoming prophets, priests, and kings — a holy nation unto the Lord.

Until God's principalities are in power and in position, all the commissioning in the world is going to be frustrated. It is the territory or jurisdiction of a prince, and in the Church, *principality* means the realm of authority and sphere of influence of an apostle.

The first Principality was God, Who is still the primary and ultimate authority. Protestants have not fully understood spiritual authority, because the Reformation fathers were so angry with the Catholic church for its unrighteous control and so fearful of continued usurpation of spiritual authority that they "threw the baby out with the bath water."

The first big schism in the Reformation was between Calvinists, who believe man has no free will at all and God does what He pleases when He pleases, and Armenians, who said God does not exercise ultimate authority over us. They say it is more like influence, which means that, in turn, the five-fold offices really are powerless in authority.

Most of the American church believes that a pastor is not really the head of the church in authority but simply a person who leads administratively and in spiritual things. People like to slide over the verse that says pastors are to "bishop," which means rule over the souls of those in their congregations. Paul said they will be held *accountable* for the souls — minds, wills, and emotions — of those assigned to them. (Hebrews 13:17.)

A recent move to restore authority ended up making "discipling" a bad word, because too many in authority were not set there by God or were not themselves under authority from God or anyone else! You must be a good follower before you can be a good leader.

As the apostle is the highest delegated office from Jesus to His Body (Ephesians 4:11), it becomes obvious that the center of principalic rule for him is the place or church where he is stationed. As an analogy, Satan is still the prince of power of the air (Ephesians 2:2), so his ruling center is the second heavens.

There are no absentee principalities. They must live in the territory of which they have been named head.

Apostles must begin in their respective houses to disseminate what brought them into their offices. The bottom line definition of *disciple* is a pupil of a founder who follows the teachings and assists in spreading them. Otherwise, you are just a follower.

Our Houses Are Not in Order

For about five years, God has kept giving me a recurring dream of a large house which has the furniture out of order. The kitchen appliances are in the bathroom, and the living room furniture is upstairs in the closet. The dining room suite is in the living room. There was something in the foyer, but I did not recognize it.

God kept showing this to me, and eventually I said, "Well, God, why?"

He said, "This is what My house looks like to Me."

The majority of Christians have no idea what their spiritual houses look like. But Satan knows. He knows that as long as *you* do not know why a living room is a living room, a dining room is a dining room, and a kitchen is a kitchen, he has power. One thing Satan has that we do not is a *clear understanding of order and the power of order.*

I have heard preachers say, "I do not know how it works, it just works. Who cares how?"

I care, because when it stops working, I want to know how to "kick it in gear" again! When things are going the right way, I want to know how to fix them. You may not care how your television works, but when it does not work, you want someone who knows how it works to fix it.

We have chosen to be like children playing in the sand box and the wading pool. We do not want to get in too deep. Do not tell us the deep things of God. But God is not going to continue to play with us in the wading pool when we ought to be adults.

Christians have been talking about "a new move," yet everything I have seen has been trying to cram the new into the old. "We always did it like that, and people liked me, so let me just do it this way." We do not like to be inconvenienced by change. We do not like to have our traditions challenged — neither did the Pharisees when Jesus came to upset their applecarts.

We do not want change if it is going to bring pain. We do not want to grow up, if it means we have to leave our toys behind. Like the Israelites in exodus from Egypt, we do not want to get free, if we have to lose the things we were enjoying in slavery.

The monolithic established church of the Dark Ages was wrong because it was tyrannical and upheld men's doctrines rather than God's Word. However, ever since the Reformation the church has been scattered in spiritual things as well as natural. We have more schisms than the tree of the knowledge of good and evil could bear! Every year there is a new schism because we have never ever understood the unity of the faith.

On the other hand, everywhere I have been lately, folks have been teaching or giving out "new" things about which I am saying, "Where did they get that, Jesus?"

And they say, "The Spirit told me." That always terrifies me, because then you have to go through this whole grocery list: Now, what spirit was this?

There is a right way in between the extremes of forced natural unity and freedom to worship as we like. We are not free to believe anything we like. We have unity in the Spirit, but we do not act like it. We must come to unity of understanding, unity in love.

If God is love, then what is He going to be moved by? What is He going to listen to? It is certainly not us criticizing one another and complaining about one another.

God is going do some tremendous things and some horrendous things in the natural, because God is making some changes. For a year, God has had me "calling forth the new," and I do not quite know what it is. Therefore, every time I did it, I could learn more.

If you do not obey the first thing God tells you, you will never understand the second. Sometimes you have to do it wrong just to get it right in the long run.

God said to me, "Tell them who I am and what I am doing in this hour."

Who Is God?

God is the Creator of heaven and earth, and you probably will say, "I know that." We all can say that, but somehow we do not believe it. God created all the heavens and all the earth. (Genesis 1.) That means every strata between heaven and earth. God created it all, as well as every spirit and every being in and between heaven and earth.

Every power that is in the earth, God created it. And every throne, and every dominion, every force, every principality, He created it. And He created His children to rule over creation. Instead, it has been ruling us.

How are we ruled by the other powers? When you tell "little white lies," and then talk about "expediency," when you make excuses for staying away from church or not witnessing to others, you are not being ruled by God. All of those things are what negate our power. We can commission people from here to the millennium, but without authority, they will have no power.

The problem with the modern Church is the same as the Pharisees had: We have "religion" without spiritual understanding. We understand, "Thou shalt not kill," we just do not recognize that you kill Jesus by "killing" others with your words.

We understand "Thou shalt not commit adultery," but to twentieth century Christians "adultery" is not sin, but a relationship, "my significant other."

We had better begin to get a clear understanding of what it means to be a disciple of Christ. The year 1996 is going to be one of judgment, but all of the judgment is not going to be bad. Some of it is going to be real, real nice.

12

1996: A Year of Judgment

Recently, I was flying home from a meeting, and I was in the back of the plane which was overcrowded. Suddenly, at my right shoulder I saw a dragon, a huge dragon who filled the air. And he had eyes of sulfur. I did not know what it was, so I had to ask God.

"Lord, what is that?"

And He said, "It is a dragon."

I said, "A what?"

He said, "A dragon. Satan himself has come for you."

I said, "Well, Lord, what do I do?"

He said, "Speak to it, and command it to leave."

I spoke to it in the Spirit, and I saw something hit it right in the stomach, and it backed away, but guess what? That only injured it. The battle is yet to come.

We are in a level and an era of God where you can kiss your comfort zone good-bye. Most of us have already experienced this.

Some of us have been so mad with God that we do not know what to do. Some of us have even written Him "hate mail."

I wrote Him a couple of letters myself: "Dear God, I am sick of the ministry. I do not like Your people. I hate Your Church. As a matter of fact, I am sick of the planet. But I love You, Paula."

I did not love the saints, and I did not love the "aint's." Not one! And you know why? Because I thought this prophetic ministry was going to be easy.

Instead, we must learn not to be one of the ways that Satan can manifest himself against someone else. You need to understand that darkness needs light to do anything. Everything you see darkness doing, it got from you and your Daddy.

In order for there to be a lie, there had to be a truth; in order for there to be death, there had to be life; in order for there to be sin, there had to be righteousness; in order for there to be failure, there had to be victory, so do not be surprised that Satan knows how to win.

We lie to ourselves when we run around singing that Satan is defeated. Positionally, Jesus defeated him at Calvary. But the fact that we have to live with is, he has not yet been run out of town.

The Church was assigned to take territory back from him. However, we have consistently not done that, and he is taking territory back from us that our forefathers took from him!

Look at him. He was on my plane. He could afford a ticket! We are the biggest and greatest weapons darkness has. It is the people who love God who frustrate His purpose and actually aid the enemy in his efforts.

It is the people who love God who rise up against Him. Those who claimed to love God are the ones who killed Jesus. It is the people who love Him who are hurting you. The people who say they love Him do not hear you cry. They love Him, but do not see your pain.

You tell many saints that you are hurting, and they will say they are going to pray for you. You know what that prayer is going be? "Thank God it is not me in that mess."

Who Are We Supposed To Be?

We exist to take the powers of darkness and put them in their subjugated place and establish the principality of light and life in creation.

We do not exist for all of the elaborate buildings.

We do not exist to show folks how much money we could raise or not raise, to decide who should preach and who should not.

We do not exist to keep the races in order.

We do not exist to rival the secular world.

We exist to eventually show everything in the universe that God was wise in creating mankind and the earth.

> To the intent that now unto the principalities and powers in heavenly places might be known by the church the manifold wisdom of God.
>
> **Ephesians 3:10**

We are the bride of Christ. We are the Great Woman. Yet the whore from Babylon (Revelation 17) has more power. We are "the woman of the house." What house? The house of creation. Yet we do not know anything about our creation. We think we are going to take on witches and warlocks, when we do not even know how they do what they do.

You are part of "the First Lady of Creation." You will never ever complete your purpose until you understand the One Who gave the purpose. Every authority we have is derived from God. That means as long as we use authority according to God's plan, it works. God is calling us to a maturity and a deliberate, effectual working of His power.

As I have heard God, what I have heard is that He is restoring *His* principalities. He is taking something and placing it in a position of arch rulership, and He is handing over the offices to the houses (churches and ministries) that He chooses.

Over the next several years, He is establishing His own apostolic houses. We have been trying to do it for Him, and I have watched people trying to do it and said, "That is not what God is doing."

He is establishing His own apostolic house and that is where this is going. I am going to tell you exactly what to expect when God's principalities are back in power. You see, we want to preach the whole Word of God but not live it.

God told me this year, "My people are going to understand there is a difference between obeying My Word and then living with that obedience."

It is easy to quit that job, but you have to live with that decision and those bills.

It is easy to say, "God called me to the ministry," but you have to live with the rejection and the resentment and all the other stuff.

We need every member of the Body doing his or her share, because when it comes to the time when the saints are going to be persecuted, it will not matter if you are a leader or a pew-sitter. To survive, we need the Body as one. We need every member full of the Holy Ghost and faith and power. We need every member prepared to stand up for Jesus.

You say, "Why are you making a big deal about 'every member'?" It is because the reason half the witches and psychics are out there operating in the world is that some church said, "God never called a woman to . . . . God never called a black person to . . . . God never called a Haitian to . . . an Asian to . . . ."

The power was in them, the call was upon them, and they had to manifest somewhere. For all of the healing we have been trying to bring to the church, we wonder why the power is not back. We have never tried to heal the breach of the genders. We do not touch that.

You see brother hugging brother, then listen to them make derogatory jokes about women in the pulpit and about how we treat our husbands. Preachers make jokes about what Affirmative Action would sue us for. But God said to tell His people to stop sabotaging themselves, to stop shooting themselves in the feet.

God is still hearing the cry of the brokenhearted. When God calls us to be a principality, you cannot use hate to beat hate. You cannot use lust to dethrone lust. The principle that Jesus gave us on the planet was, "A house divided against itself cannot stand." (Matthew 12:25.) How can Satan cast out Satan?

We want to win the lost of the world, yet we make it public that we do not like this group or will not accept that group, and if you come to our church, you have to act like this.

Why is judgment coming down on the house of God? It is because we have forgotten our mandate. We have forgotten that Paul laid out the gifts of the Spirit and talked of "faith, hope, and charity (love)," but said, **the greatest of these is charity** (1 Corinthians 13:13).

We Have Forgotten Our Mandate

We have forgotten that Jesus' mandate also is ours:

> **The Spirit of the Lord is upon me, because he hath anointed me to preach the gospel to the poor; he hath sent me to heal the brokenhearted, to preach deliverance to the captives, and recovering of sight to the blind, to set at liberty them that are bruised, to preach the acceptable year of the Lord.**
>
> **Luke 4:18,19**

People are not in the house of God, because we have not made it attractive. We have made it very difficult, or very embarrassing, or very humiliating, or very unpleasant. They get more people at a motivation conference than we get in church.

We somehow read this verse as a statement instead of a question.

> **How should one chase a thousand, and two put ten thousand to flight, except their Rock had sold them, and the Lord had shut them up?**
>
> **Deuteronomy 32:30**

We are not going to win this thing being like the world.

Many of the people God is going to be using will offend our religious sensibilities. Many will be the same ones you saw on television "humping and bumping." He is going to use them because they are not tainted, not already fixed in their views.

It is going to be the base things — the folks no one likes, the folks everyone overlooks — who will do the greatest works. *True saith God the Lord*
Look at 1 Corinthians 1:27-29:

> **But God hath chosen the foolish things of the world to confound the wise; and God hath chosen the weak things of the world to confound the things**

which are mighty; And base things of the world, and
things which are despised, hath God chosen, yea, and
things which are not, to bring to nought things that
are: That no flesh should glory in his presence.

The Prophetic Precedes the Apostolic

We also need to realize that the prophetic move
always precedes the apostolic. The reason we see a lot
of flurry going on now in the area of the prophetic and
apostolic is because God has ordained the restoration.
And people can smell power.

However, God is saying to us in this hour that, "If
you are going to be used by Me, you are not going to be
used according to your plan and your standard."

Jesus said you have to cast out the strong man
before you can plunder his house. Satan is still operating, even if he has been defeated by Jesus, because we
were just "kicking back," not walking in our authority.

In order to displace the "strong man," you must
have three things from the Source of all power and
authority: God's authority, God's instructions and
directions, and God's approval. Otherwise, the strong
man will go after you.

And I hear the Holy Spirit saying to us, as we
go on, that God is raising up apostolic houses that are
literally going to be set in the heavenlies. Yet it will not
be obvious to the natural eye, because the ones He sets
in office will walk in humility.

No proper "governor" in the Kingdom will operate out from under submission to the Principality over
him. In true apostolic servants, you will see God's power
roll out over the earth.

God says time is short. He does not have time to
wait for us to start agreeing with Him, or to start seeing

the wisdom of His plan. He will not do the obvious in this move. That is why much of what He has been doing lately has not made sense. We are trying to measure Him according to the obvious.

King David's favorite son, Absalom, was so sure he was the man for the new move. He ordered the hall, had his cooks lay on a great feast, hired singers and minstrels, had new robes made, and sent out invitations to his coronation.

Absalom was so obvious that people did not even check with God. He was an obvious replacement. He had a prominent ministry. He looked kingly and walked like one in authority.

But who ascended the throne? A son who was not so well-known, the boy whose mother got her husband killed. The boy whose mother committed adultery. His story is something like that of Jesus. He was born, then the next time you hear about him, he is ascending the throne. Sounds like God to me.

Solomon was not at the party, he did not even get an invitation. He was never in the gates with Absalom, as Absalom was passing judgments, slinging his beautiful hair around. (2 Samuel 14:26.)

Where was Solomon? He was with David, the king. Solomon was sitting down getting the plans and writing them out. Solomon was back at the house, listening to the wisdom of the ages, while Absalom was acting to take his "proper" place by force.

Solomon never pushed himself forward, he just let God do it in His own time. I am sure Absalom must have mocked Solomon all the time. It is so phenomenal how God used Solomon, showing us that your earthly heritage does not count against you with God.

Bathsheba was in the lineage of Jesus; however, God deleted her name. God is really unhappy with you when He does not even want to call you by name, but by a pronoun. In Matthew, she is listed as "*her* who had been the wife of Uriah."

We have Absalom movements going on right now in the Church. You do not have to do anything, just have a visible ministry, and some people will say, "We'll come to the banquet hall, we'll make you a robe, we'll make you a miter, we'll buy you a ring."

These movements may look like God but what is lacking is God's plan. We are told that, because some have been made bishops, that makes them an apostle. Not so. *Every apostle is a bishop, but not every bishop is an apostle.* Most bishops have to answer to their denominations or their people. Apostles only answer to God.

We need to recognize that the Absalom movement always precedes the coronation of Solomon. There is a great fanfare with all these people standing around cheering over you. Then you have to build yourself a little wooden throne, because the real throne went to Solomon.

God sends forerunners, like John the Baptist, to prepare the way for His moves. And the devil usually sees that and begins his own counterfeit, trying to usurp God's institution of the real thing.

As God puts His powers in place, you are going to see the Holy Spirit begin to manifest — and it is not going to be a pretty picture — because you are going to see men of power act like kids who try to keep their toys away from other kids.

You will see them having closed meetings and daring their people to talk to this one or that one, even threatening them with being ostracized and with "excommunication." Why? Because power is a heady thing.

How To Tell the False From the True

How can you know the difference between the false and the true? The first way is by the Spirit, as Anna and Simeon knew the baby Jesus was Messiah (Luke 2:25-38), the second, by their fruits (Luke 6:44), and thirdly, because the false always comes first and with fanfare.

When Jesus was crowned King of kings and Lord of lords, no one knew it.

When you have not put your ear to God's heart, you too will elevate the wrong ones, you will submit to the wrong ones, you will let the wrong ones in your house. We are going to see many more marches in which born-again, Spirit-filled men filled with all the power of the Godhead will participate.

Men who have an eternal covenant with God will bow to the god of the dead. Absalom is going to invite you to the banquet hall. He is going send you a glossy invitation engraved in gold for a front row seat.

He is going to say, "I am the new king. Did you not get the news? Well, you probably were not listening to God."

If you sit down there to his dainty delicacies, while his food is in your mouth and the delusion is in your head, the trumpets will sound. "Solomon" will rise, and he has the plan.

Many Christians will have to back out in embarrassment and go to Solomon and say, "I do not know what happened. It looked like God, it felt like God, it sounded like God, but obviously, it was not God."

The seed is cursed when you break your covenant with the God of the covenant. Your children are not suffering because of any white man, green man, or orange man. Your children are suffering because your daddies broke their covenant with the most high God.

The plan for bringing the family back together is not Islam. Louis Farrakhan is dividing blacks from their Christian heritage, from their Redeemer, from their spouses and children. He is not bringing black men together. His movement is the "Absolom" movement standing in the gates with great fanfare.

Every time he stood up to speak in the recent "Million Man March," he gave credit to his god. Also, he stood up as a prophet. That means he exercised the spiritual authority of a prophet and offered those men to "Allah." And every spirit attending Farrakahn on that march received a vessel. You think Christians are the only ones able to impart? We are not the only ones.

In order to be principalities under God, we have to take back certain things, which we have lost one by one:

1. The first is spiritual authority.

2. The second is supernatural power.

3. The next control is influence in the government.

4. The fourth control is education.

5. The next is the airways, because you must seize the ears, the eyes and the hearts of the people.

6. Before all of this taking back, we have to take back the Church.

Until we do that, God's not moving those principalities Paul wrote about, those authorities of Satan. You are going to see more and more cult shows on the air and more and more cult activity. You are going to see witches continue to teach your children and ease their teachings into your children's textbooks.

Satan's officials have gained all that territory, because we let them do it. We voted for free expression at any cost. We are the only army that sabotages our commission. In armies of the world, they call that treason and shoot you for it.

God wants us to get used to "taking care of business" for Him. He wants us to become accustomed to handling these things. Most of us cannot give an answer concerning what hope is in us, because we do not know for sure what it is. We think it is getting "raptured" out of the earth.

However, we are God's principality of light and life on the planet. Without us, this thing is gone. We are the authority, speaking for Jesus, that is to tell darkness to flee. We are the power that looses finances and healing.

We have the authority over all power of the enemy, because Jesus delegated His authority to us. We are the power that tells cancer to get out of your body and the thief to restore seven-fold. We have spiritual command, and the spiritual is always higher than the natural.

If you believe that you are commissioned, then you need to know that not only do you have great responsibility, you have even greater resources. Remember, however, that God is not casting out any of those principalities we have been fighting until we are ready to take their places.

Part Six
Shall Not a People Seek Their God?

by Carlton Pearson

13

There Is No Light in Them

We are a nation, a people, desperate today to hear a word from the other world, the supernatural realm.

Many people involved in astrology and the occult have no idea it is evil. They have no idea what a familiar spirit is, or a medium, or a spiritist, or a wizard.

God is going to judge that whole operation in this nation and around the world this year. Part of it is fake, but the rest is *divination*. The Greek word is *putho*, from which we get "python." Many people are innocently and ignorantly engaging in practices involving these things and have no idea what they are giving entrance to in their lives.

At Higher Dimensions Church, we help people every day and on an ongoing basis who are dealing with various occultic oppressions in their minds. They come for prayer and counselling, and write letters to us from across this country.

The Bible tells us in many passages not to become involved in the occult. One of those places is Isaiah 8:19-22 NIV:

> When men tell you to consult mediums and spiritists, who whisper and mutter, *should not a people inquire of their God?* Why consult the dead on behalf of the living? To the law and to the testimony! If they

do not speak according to this word, they have no light
of dawn. **Distressed and hungry, they will roam
through the land; when they are famished, they will
become enraged and, looking upward, will curse their
king and their God. Then they will look toward the
earth and see only distress and darkness and fearful
gloom, and** *they will be thrust into utter darkness.*

"Familiar spirits" is the Hebrew word *owb*, or
obe, a derivative of *ab*, the Hebrew word for "father,"
apparently with the idea of "prattling a father's name."
(We might pray over and over, "Abba Father. Daddy
God.")

Isaiah was saying that contacting familiar spirits is
"prattling" or whispering the name of Satan or some of
his lesser followers, such as Baal, over and over as an
incantation. Transcendentalism and other Eastern cults
are noted for repetition of certain "mantras," or phrases.
Most of them have no idea they are, in essence, calling
out to the devil as father.

A *mutter*, or *mumble* is from the Hebrew word for
a water skin, found in the same root word as *obe*, and
associated with familiar spirits. It means "hollow," from
the sound of hitting on a water bottle.

Water bottles in Egypt and the Middle East were
animal skins made into bags or sacks in which liquids
could be carried. From the hollow sound also came the
term, *necromancer*, or "one who communicates with the
dead." Today, we call them *mediums, spiritists,* or
channelers. In Bible days, they were known as those who
"mutter."

Do you know what the word "jinx" means that
has become a word for bad luck? It was a bird used in
casting magical spells — "peep-chirp," etc.

Another associated word for "those who peep and
mutter" is *ventriloquist* as one whose voice issues from

a jar or a bottle. The voice is projected in such a manner that the sound appears to come from a source other than the vocal organs of the speaker.

The person through whom familiar spirits speak is like a puppet or a mere tool, a doll, a mannequin, an imitation, a sham, or a forgery. An imitation is something likely to be mistaken for something of higher value. It is insincere, not genuine. The Bible speaks of judgment on those kinds of things and on people who practice them.

Some organizations of which people are not aware fall into this category, organizations that on the surface would seem to have nothing to do with the occult.

For example, the Ku Klux Klan (KKK) began as a secret society established by white Protestant ex-Confederate soldiers. Taking into consideration the spirituality of the freed slaves, they set out to frighten blacks out of taking part in society and government.

They put on the white hood and the white robe to symbolize Confederate soldiers, slave owners, or slave overseers come back from the dead to haunt the slaves in their freedom. It is a cult, and it is occultish. The word *occult* simply means "mystery or secret."

The word *wizard*, even the Grand or Imperial Wizard, is from the Hebrew word *yidd oniy*, or "knowing one," and that comes from the root word *yada*, meaning "to know." Remember Yoda in Star Wars? That is a derivation of the Hebrew word. Steven Spielburg was expressing through his name the character of the guy with the pointed ears, the little guy who was the "all-knowing one."

Yoda was a "conjurer." The literal word, *yada*, in Hebrew means "to ascertain by observation," in this case, by observing the world of the occult.

Anything that has a secret, private oath is considered in the category of occultism. As God flexes His muscle against those kinds of spirits, you will begin to see great unrest, upheaval and confusion, including suicides, imprisonments, and infighting among the cults and those involved in psychic hotlines and other forms of occultism. Notice the headlines the rest of 1996 and beyond.

Prophets and Familiar Spirits Are "Mouthpieces"

Essentially, those who contact spirits, whatever they are called, act as mouthpieces for demons and/or Satan. They are counterfeits of prophets, who speak for God. The difference is that Satan's "voices" usually are taken over by him, sooner or later, and have no choice in what they do. Most of them also are deluded and deceived, because he and his spirits lie to them.

Prophets are called by God to speak for Him and can choose. The Bible says the spirit of a prophet is subject to the prophet. (1 Corinthians 14:32.) God does not "possess" His voices and override their choices.

The first mention of a prophet in the Old Testament is in reference to Abraham. The word actually means "inspired man, or inspired person." A prophet was not the same as a *seer*, which is simply "one who sees the future," a see-er. A biblical prophet was a person who spoke for God, sometimes in literal words from God.

Their utterances were God-breathed, Holy Spirit-inspired. They were enthusiasts for God, mouthpieces for the Almighty on earth. The word *enthusiasm* comes from "in *theos*," as God breathes through you. That is the root of our word "theology." A prophecy was an inspired song or saying, an inspired discourse, a story, a word, a tale. It was something that had come forth under the divine inspiration of the Holy Ghost.

Why Are People Looking for Words?

Now, why are people in the rationalistic 90s seeking for words from spirits? It is because they want to be satisfied, ratified, and gratified. They want approval. They want to be approved or improved, when sometimes they need to be reproved. When the Church allowed American society to begin to "retire" God to the sidelines, people began to look for something else to fill the spiritual void.

Even Christians can feel the world shaking in all of its systems and literally in a nation. They also are looking for security, for a sense there is someone to lean on, someone who is really confident and positive, to tell them what to do. Many of them do not get this anymore in their churches. As in Jesus' time, even many preachers do not "speak with authority." There is instability on this earth. People are very insecure.

Christians will pack out a place, if they think they are going to get "a word from the Lord." And prophets prophesy to each other. They are trying to hear God, too. Sometimes they can hear God for you, and cannot hear for themselves.

However, it is not a long, drawn out sermon that does the ministry — it is a certain spirit, a certain intonation, a certain Presence that your soul absorbs. God wants you to have your own personal, individual, intimate relationship with Him, through Jesus Christ. I am not the source. I am not God's substitute in your life, neither are any of the true prophets.

Many church-going people are not born again, but are just religious. They are religious because they are afraid, but true Christianity is not built on fear. It is built upon hope, on faith, and on a loving relationship with a living God.

If true Christians really knew what a prophetic word — an inspired word from God — is, they could prophesy to themselves, to their children, prophesy to their spouses, even to their finances or their businesses. Let your words be inspired of God! God desires that His people walk in divine inspiration all the time. Everything you say, everything you do should be inspired.

I want to be anointed even when I am correcting my son.

I want to be inspired in a meaningful conversation with my wife. I want our conversation to be inspirational.

Everyone Is Looking for Answers

When the Lord spoke through Isaiah about people saying "Seek unto them that have familiar spirits," the word *seek* is the word *darash* in Hebrew. It means "to tread or to frequent, to take as a route, or as a means of transportation, a means of travel, a means of progress."

He was saying, "When people tell you to follow after or to search, ask, inquire of, or make inquisition or inquiry, to question or examine or study, consult or counsel" with familiar spirits," then you ask them why not seek God for answers.

This is what is going on with the psychic hotlines today.

People are saying, "Why don't you seek those who can tell you the future? Call the hotline and find the answer to your problems."

In actuality, whether they know it or not, they are saying, "Call those people who peep and mutter, those who commune with familiar spirits," or supposedly with the devil.

But are we saying, "Should not a people seek their God?" Or are we letting them go down the road to destruction?

Remember the tree of knowledge of good and evil in the Garden of Eden? The tree that Adam and Eve were forbidden to eat of, but did. (Genesis 2:17.) The word *knowledge* there is *da'ath* in Hebrew, and it means "cunning or experienced," the tree of experimentation, the tree of awareness.

In other words, God said, "I don't want you to eat or live by knowledge possible to man by his own reasoning, his own logic, his own computation, his own rationale and surmisings, his own experience, conclusions, or calculations — outside of divine revelation from Me."

There is a direct link here between the first words of God recorded in Scripture, **Let there be light** (Genesis 1:3), and the prohibition against eating of the one tree.

Let there be illumination.

Let there be revelation.

Let there be light from darkness.

Let there be divinely ordained perception.

> **And the earth was without form, and void; and darkness was upon the face of the deep. And the Spirit of God moved upon the face of the waters. And God said, Let there be light: and there was light.**
>
> **Genesis 1:2,3**

Sin has to do with your perception. The Greek word for sin is *harmartia*, which literally means "to miss the mark, to miss the target, to miss your aim." *Mark* is from the Greek word *scopos*, where we get the English word "scope."

Jesus said we would "tread on scorpions (the Greek word *scorpios*) and serpents" (Luke 10:19), which ties into the references to Satan as a serpent in Genesis. In fact, the Greek word for "serpent" is *ophis*, which comes from *ophthalmos*, which is where we get our English word "opthamology." However, *ophis* literally means "sharpness of vision," "a type of sly cunning," or "an artful, enchanting, or malicious person."

The words for serpent, familiar spirits, and natural vision all seem to relate to the concept in Genesis of the tree of knowledge of good and evil relating to man's knowledge, the way man perceives life and creation. Obviously, the way man sees, "by sight and not by faith," (2 Corinthians 5:7) is opposite to divine revelation, or the way God perceives, which is the true and accurate way things are.

Paul wrote that if the truth is hidden from the world, it is because "the god of this world" has blinded their eyes. (2 Corinthians 4:4.) In other words, many people cannot see the truth about God because they "see" the same way the serpent conned Eve into perceiving.

> But if our gospel be hid, it is hid to them that are lost: In whom the god of this world hath blinded the minds of them which believe not, lest the light of the glorious gospel of Christ, who is the image of God, should shine unto them.
>
> 2 Corinthians 4:3,4

When you are blind to the light of the Gospel, then sin issues forth in adultery, stealing, lying, murder, and all of the related ways in which the Ten Commandments are broken. However, the primary sin any human being commits is to fall short of the glory, the clearness, clarity, transparency, or translucence of God — the purity, clarity and truth of God's Word.

There are some more associations between vision, the serpent, and man's knowledge. Genesis 3:1 says the serpent was more "subtle" than any of the other "beasts of the field." The Hebrew word for *subtle* is *aruwm*, meaning "cunning (usually in a bad sense), crafty, prudent." Again, it is interesting that *naked* is from the same root, almost the same word, *arowm*, or *arom*. It has the connotation of "smoothness and slipperiness." When the serpent said, "If you eat of the forbidden tree, you will not die but instead will become like God," he was speaking partial truth but mostly a lie. *Nakedness* and *subtlty* are almost synonymous derivations. The serpent's intention was to make Eve and ultimately Adam not to become like God, but instead, to become like himself — slick and crafty.

There is something else we need to see in the story of mankind's beginning, and that is what kind of serpent Moses was writing about.

A Serpent's Hiss Gets Attention

If there is one thing that will get anyone's attention, it is "Psst! Psst!" You could be in a place where there is loud music or people shouting, when someone nearby goes "Psst," and you will turn around and say, "What?" Why do we connect hissing with the devil? It is because of the descriptions of him as a serpent in Eden.

There are three Hebrew words in the Old Testament used for serpent: *nachash, tanniyn* or *tan*, and *saraph.*

Nachash is the word used to describe the serpent in Eden. It would help Christians understand the Bible better if they knew that names did not used to be "labels." All of the ancient names either were a description, a function, or a related association of people or things.

Like the Native Americans, our ancient ancestors used names to tell something. Take *Abraham*, for example. His name meant "father of multitudes." Whenever anyone spoke to the man, he was saying, "Oh, father of multitudes." His birthname, Abram, literally meant "high father."

The Israelites were inspired in naming their children in many cases, calling them whatever they were to be or to be like.

When Moses called the serpent *Nachash*, he was describing it. The root word means "to hiss or whisper a magic spell or incantation." Moses was telling us that the devil took over a snake that hissed. Later, when Moses fashioned a brass serpent to hold up for the Israelites to look upon and be healed from the bites of fiery serpents, this is the word used.

The second word, *tan*, means "an elongated, unusually large monster," so *tanniym* was a sea serpent, a whale, or a dragon. It is interesting that when God turned the rod into a serpent to prove to the Israelites He had sent Moses, it was "a serpent that hissed," but when Moses threw the same rod down for Pharaoh, it turned into a "tanniym," a large sea monster. The magicians' rods also became these larger snakes.

The third kind of snake, *saraph*, is the word God used in telling Moses to fashion the brass fiery serpent; however, when Moses did put the symbol up on a pole, it is called *nachash*. God was describing the serpent, because *saraph* means "to be set on fire," "burning," or "coppery," from its color and its bite. This was a poisonous serpent found in the wilderness.

By the time Greek became the predominant language, there was only one word for serpent used in the Bible, *ophis*, having to do with vision, cunning, and artfulness. To be crafty, one has to have a certain amount of discernment, one has to be able to see motivations and manipulative possibilities that the average person does not see.

Also, one who had a spirit of divination as did the girl who followed Paul around was called *pulon*, "a gateway to *puthon*, or "the python." However, the word did not come from the python snake but from the name of a town in Greece, Putho, where a spirit called "the Delphic oracle" prophesied out of a wind or breeze blowing from a cave.

Nevertheless, the point is that in the original wording of Scripture, there is a relationship found all the way through the Bible between Satan as a serpent, the way we see the world (our mindsets or worldviews), and divination, or communicating with Satan.

Snakes are fascinating to watch, as long as they are in a zoo or behind glass! Have you ever looked into a serpent's eyes? You can easily believe a connection between reptiles and the devil. People will stop in front of them and go, "Ooh! Ooh! Ahh!"

That is happening now with the occult. The serpents are out there hissing and whispering, appealing to the part of man that doubts God, and biting with fiery poison those who get near enough to grab.

I have never felt such an intensity to touch God as I do as we hit the final years of the 90s. I have a desire to seek God as never before, to call upon Him, to inquire of Him, to pray, to examine my own relationship with Him, and to find out more about who God really is. Of course, you will never really know who God is until you meet His Son, Jesus.

Jesus came to say, "Let Me show you what God is really like. I come from the Father, I say and do only what I see the Father do. When you see Me, you see the Father. When you hear Me, you have heard the Father. When you hear the Father, He is speaking through Me." (John 14:9.)

The bottom line, after all the dust settles is: *What are you going to do with Jesus?*

14

Satan Always Speaks Twice

The enemy never comes and speaks once, then leaves. He speaks repeatedly until he convinces you or you kick him out for good. He comes back subtly and insidiously again and again, hissing his incantations into your spiritual ear.

Satan did not just find Eve that first day and she went, "Ahhh!" and ate the apple. He kept "pastoring" her. The word *pastor/shepherd* is from the Hebrew *ra'ah*, which means "to tend a flock, or to pasture it." However, it also means "evil entreaty" and "shepherd," among related definitions. In the New Testament, it is the Greek word *polmen*.

As I mentioned earlier, prophets and seers were not always the same. Some prophets also were seers, but some were not. Some disagree with this distinction today; however, the Bible makes it clear there were two separate functions.

> Yet the Lord testified against Israel, and against Judah, by all the prophets, and by all the seers, saying, Turn ye from your evil ways, and keep my commandments and my statutes, according to all the law which I commanded your fathers, and which I sent to you by my servants the prophets.
>
> 2 Kings 17:13

The law was given by the prophets, God's mouth-pieces and servants, but some warnings or prophesies — the Lord's testimony that would prove His people deserved judgment — were given through seers, those who saw what was coming in the future.

There also were seers in the land not receiving their vision from God. They were looking through crystal balls and cards, and throwing animal entrails on the ground and prognosticating the future by the way they fell, something like reading tea leaves today.

They were using rocks and trees in their "scrying" attempts to see the future. When we see the word "God" in the Old Testament, most of the time the Hebrew word is *Elohiym*, transliterated into the English *Elohim*. It comes from *El*, which means "strength" and from *eyil*, which means a strong support, or an oak or other strong tree.

The tree was where Adam and Eve got their first meal that was not of God. Before that, they could eat all of the other fruits, grains, and vegetables. This is why many people in various cultures worship trees. Handed down in their cultures is the idea that a tree was the cause of the world's being the way it is. So trees have been elevated or mistaken for God.

In the Middle and Far East, you will see trees with roots that wrap around and around, almost looking like serpents coming up out of the ground. The cypress trees growing out of swamps in the deep South also have twisted roots. Many witch groups and cults worship trees and have extended that cultic worship now to the earth itself. They have named the earth, Gaia, after an ancient goddess.

Witchcraft often takes place in the woods and in the forests, around the trees. We build with the tree.

Staffs, rods, or canes represent a branch that comes from a tree. You lean on the staff, you walk with a staff. A scepter which represented authority in some cases was a wooden rod.

An "office staff" is the same meaning once removed. They support the boss, or the leader as he walks, talks, and works.

Witchcraft, psychic hotlines, horoscopes, that stuff has a certain reality to it — but it is very, very dangerous. It is like a drug, once it gets its hooks in you, you cannot come out without some assistance from the Holy Spirit.

I have a feeling the serpent, the initial serpent in his elongated state, looked something like a tree. He was tall and attractive, and his hissing incantations appealed to the natural appetite of Eve, and she conceded.

Now let's look at one more connection between our problems today that involve our worldviews — the way we see ourselves and God — the New Age and occult, and all of the drug and addictive substance problems that have increased tremendously since World War I.

A sorcerer was called a *magos*, hence the wise men who came to worship Jesus as a baby in Bethlehem often are referred to as Magi. Not all Magi of the East were sorcerers or magicians in the sense of satanic connections, however.

In the book of Revelation, when John wrote that no *sorcerers* would enter the gates of the Holy City, the word is *pharmakos*. This word comes from *pharmakeia, pharmakeus* and *pharmakon*. These are Greek words from which we get the English words for pharmacy, pharmaceutical, druggist or pharmacist (by extension, a "magician"). Sometimes these words are translated "witchcraft" or "magic."

Sorcery originally had to do with drugs and potions in a perversion of God's herbs of the earth provided for our health and of the leaves of the heavenly tree that are for the healing of the nations.

If we want people to hear God and not all of these satanic counterfeits, we must teach them that God is easily approachable. They do not need hotlines, tea leaves, tree worship, and muttering and peeping mantras.

God Is Not in the Dramatic

When Moses went up to the mountain to receive the Ten Commandments, the people were afraid to go up with him. So they remained behind and got into trouble over having Aaron build a golden calf, an idol to worship instead of God.

They said, "Please do not let God speak to us, Moses, *you* speak to us." (Exodus 20:19.) God can be very dramatic, although usually He is not. There was vapor and smoke. The mountain was quaking, and there was wind. Exodus 20:18 says:

> And all the people saw the thunderings, and the lightnings, and the noise of the trumpet, and the mountain smoking: and when the people saw it, they removed, and stood afar off.

God knows that we generally are not interested in the subject matter, so He comes with smoke and vapor and stuff. Mature Christians who are walking in God and able to recognize the anointing do not have to have a lot of fanfare. But most of us are not mature.

> And they said unto Moses, Speak thou with us, and we will hear: but let not God speak with us, lest we die.
>
> **Exodus 20:19**

The only prophet we see in the Bible prior to this is Abraham. He was a prophet in the ancient sense. We never hear of him prophesying in the sense of giving forth the word of the Lord directly or in oracles of the future.

However, he was enthusiastic about God and showed forth the doings of the Lord to his neighbors and family. His children's children until today even know of God through the prophet and patriarch Abraham.

How do we know he was a prophet then, a mouthpiece for God? We know it because God Himself said it. When God rebuked Abimelech for taking Sarah into his harem thinking she was Abraham's sister, He told the ruler that Abraham was his prophet.

Here was a prophet who lied in a sense. Sarah was his father's child, not his mother's. However, he compromised the truth. Although Abimelech acted innocently, God closed up the wombs of all his household for Abraham's sake. In Genesis 20:7, God intervened for Abraham's sake and also for Abimelech, who had not intended to do wrong, being ignorant of Sarah's real status.

Now therefore restore the man his wife; for he is a prophet, and he shall pray for thee, and thou shalt live....

The second time you see the word *prophet* in Scripture is in reference to Aaron. Moses argued that he could not talk to Pharaoh because he was not an orator and had a speech impediment. Although God's "anger was kindled" against Moses for his reluctance to move, He sent Moses' brother Aaron, who was an eloquent speaker, with him. (Exodus 4:14-16.)

God said Aaron would be Moses' "mouthpiece," his prophet. God would speak to Moses, then Moses instead of God would speak to Aaron. Aaron would then speak to the Israelites and to Pharaoh for Moses. In Exodus 7:1, God said:

> ...See, I have made thee a god to Pharaoh: and Aaron thy brother shall be thy prophet.

In order for Pharaoh to truly hear, however, God had to send plagues that turned the Egyptians' primary gods on them. They worshipped insects, they got insects. They worshipped frogs, they got frogs, and so forth. God sometimes has to allow dramatic things to take place to get people's attention, even to His own servants.

When Elijah was running from Jezebel and hiding in the cave, begging God to kill him (1 Kings 19:4), God said, "Come out here, I want to show you something." (1 Kings 19:11-13.)

A "great and strong wind" blew that tore open mountains and broke rocks in pieces, but God said, "I am not in the blowing of the wind."

The earth quaked, and God said, "I am not in the earthquake."

And then came a fire, but God was not in fire.

Finally, there came a still small voice, and Elijah knew that was God.

We see God's dramatic displays of power again, but where was God? He was not in the dramatics, but above them causing the manifestations. He was the still small voice heard in the lull after the storm.

Where is the still small voice that is speaking in your heart? God's not into the dramatics — He will use it — but that is not His nature.

We must not be like the Egyptians and look to the spirit world of Satan for our answers. We must not look *to* dramatics for God.

We must not be like the Israelites who were too afraid to follow God all the way and were put off by the dramatics.

Christians must be ready to go all the way, to "stay the distance, and hear the still, small voice of God for direction and guidance.

From all of these word connections that I have painstakingly drawn, we can see our problems today are simply amplifications of what Satan did in the Garden of Eden with Eve: Communicating with him instead of God, looking at creation and scientific things from his viewpoint instead of God's, and participating in unwholesome and ungodly entertainments and substances.

People Need God, Not Psychics

People do not need fortune-tellers and psychics, they need God to breathe on them, to them, and through them. They need Jesus in their hearts making them new creatures and the Holy Spirit removing the "scales" off their eyes to see that Jesus really is God the Son.

They do not just need preachers, teachers and evangelists to show them the light, but they need apostles to restore order out of satanic darkness and chaos. They need prophets to give them inspired words from God, the heavenly Father and Creator of all things.

We have to know what we believe, why we believe, who we are, and where we are going, or we will not make the next few years victoriously. There is only one God — and He expressed Himself on this earth for thirty-three and one-half years, through His Son, Jesus

Christ. Now that Son is glorified, or clarified, by the Holy Ghost, Who is not around us but in us when we accept Jesus!

Part Seven
Practicing What We Preach

by Charles Dixon

15

Wake Up and Smell the Coffee!

I believe American Christians must "wake up and smell the coffee." Other groups are doing what we only preach. We need to give water to the thirsty and food to the hungry. Hurting people see too many church folks wearing nice clothes, driving beautiful cars, but never so much as handing out a cookie to those in need.

In Matthew 25, Jesus' words about the judgment are recorded, with some very sad consequences for some who have thought they were following Him:

> Then shall he say also unto them on the left hand, Depart from me, ye cursed, into everlasting fire, prepared for the devil and his angels: For I was an hungred, and ye gave me no meat: I was thirsty, and ye gave me no drink: I was a stranger, and ye took me not in: naked, and ye clothed me not: sick, and in prison, and ye visited me not.

Verses 41-43

They will ask, "Lord, when did we see You hungry, and we did not come to You? When did we see You naked? When did we see You in prison?"

And Jesus will answer:

> ...Inasmuch as ye did it not to one of the least of these, ye did it not to me.

Verse 45

We can win the world for Jesus, if we will quit being selfish and self-centered.

In the meantime, that gap of reaching out in love to help those less fortunate is being filled by Islam and other ungodly groups. God is calling Christians to release His love into our communities, to demonstrate to the world who Jesus is and that we are His.

As Christians, we must stop living by experience and learn to live up to our potential if we are to win the world. As a matter of fact, prophets are anointed to speak personal prophecies concerning a person's potential — not speak to his experience.

When Samuel anointed David, he spoke to the youth's potential. (1 Samuel 16:1-13.) However, first he reviewed David's seven brothers, thinking each was surely the one to be anointed. All were good-looking, strong men. Yet God chose the youngest, a mere youth still looking after the family sheep in the hills around Bethlehem.

Samuel told Jesse to line up all the big boys. We always see in the flesh and look in the flesh for leaders and heroes. We look first at the guy who pumps iron, whose biceps are like Charles Atlas.

God said, "No, and no, and no," right down the line from one to seven.

The prophet probably was thinking, "My God, have I missed it?"

How many times has God spoken to you, but at first it did not seem to work, and you thought you had missed Him?

However, God had told Samuel not to choose by the looks or the heights of those young men, because

the Lord seeth not as man seeth. (v. 7.) How does God see? He looks on the heart.

So Samuel looked at Jesse and said, "Jesse, please say yes. Do you have one more son?"

He said, "Yes," and Samuel said, "Go get him!"

So someone rushed out to the field where David was with the sheep and brought him into Bethlehem. David was not as tall as his brothers, Jewish history tells us, but he was "of a beautiful countenance and good to look at," the Bible says.

The only difference between him and his brothers apparently was the state of his heart. What happened? Like Samuel, we tend to look first at the outward person, at what *is*, not what can be, as God sees.

God said to Samuel, "Rise up and anoint him."

And he anointed David and prophesied to David, who at that time, probably smelled like a sheep. He was not wearing a three-piece suit, and did not have a degree behind his name. He was only a teenager, but the prophet of God spoke to his potential, and not to his experience.

God said, in essence, "You smell like a sheep and look like a sheep, and you are going to shepherd My people." David had the heart, and at that time, that was all the attribute he had toward being a king.

Jesse was no king, so David was no king by birth. But a man of God, a prophet of God, saw something in his spirit and anointed a youth from the backwoods, who became the greatest king Israel ever had from a spiritual standpoint. Only his son, Solomon, was greater from a natural standpoint.

Some people receive a word from God, and when nothing happens right away, get frustrated and cause something to happen on their own. They birth an "Ishmael." They lose out, because they wanted the thing to be done right now.

However, no prophecy will come to pass if you do not work with God. Prophecy is a signpost pointing in a certain direction, not an end in itself. It is a road map, not the car nor the destination. As a young man, David worked for God from a pure heart, doing what God brought him to do, and Samuel's prophecies came to pass after a number of years.

Prophecy should not be an end in itself. You have to seek the face of God.

The Bible said, "If you seek Me with all your heart, you will find Me." (Psalm 119:2.)

God wants you to do your homework. God wants you to prioritize Jesus! Do not lean on the arm of the prophet!

Psychic Is Not Prophetic

Even Christians are taking their tithes and offerings to call psychics. They want someone to give them a "quick fix" for their problems.

Christians, it is dangerous to rely on anyone else to hear God for you, even a most respected prophet. If God wants to tell you something you have not been able to hear, He will use a prophet. But it is not a good idea to run around hunting "words from the Lord" as so many are doing today.

Getting to know the voice of God for yourself is a daily walk. There is a price to pay, a dying to self, and a godly walk to walk. In the spirit realm, do not be in a haste to move. Be still and know that He is God. Build a relationship with your heavenly Father so that you will personally know His voice.

Many think, "Oh, well, it's only words. It can't hurt me."

I beg your pardon, oh, yes, it can! God is not the only one who can impart something to you. Once it comes from the devil, it is something released, and it is a python.

You think, "Oh, I got a false word, and a false word wouldn't hurt me."

No! The false word *may* hurt you!

That "word" from the psychic imparts demons. Like scorpions or snakes, that thing imparted may lay dormant for a while. Sooner or later, it will rear its head and fasten its fangs into you or sting you. In either case, you will have received poison from the enemy.

Eventually, that python will circle around you. You see, when he is doing it, you do not feel it until it begins to suck the juice, the life out of you. And it will leave venom, a poison in you. And that poison will eventually swell you up.

A lot of people are going to psychics and being bitten by a python which eventually may squeeze them to death.

"I called, and they told me I was going to marry such-and-such a person. That was just fun. It does not mean anything. I am not going out looking for someone of that description."

Anything from the devil eventually is going to destroy you. If it is nothing but pride that swells you up.

That is why when Paul was bitten by a snake when he was shipwrecked on the island of Melita, he threw it into the fire. He got the venom away from him as soon as possible. (Acts 28:3-5.)

Or the "venom" might have gotten into him whispering, "Paul, you are a great man. You are an awesome man. You are the man of God for the hour."

The poison will get into you, and pride comes before a fall. Venomous words are coming from the psychic lines and biting people. Many are hanging onto those words, and they are swelling them up.

No one man is "the man of God" for the hour. Jesus is the man of God for the hour! It is very sad that, when psychics "came out of the closet," it seems that Christians went in!

I believe it is time for the prophets, the prophetic churches, and the prophetic company of people to come out of the closet. If we really believe Jesus is coming soon, we should understand it is time for a company of prophets to rise up crying repentance and prepare the way.

At a conference in 1985, I gave a prophet of God the word of the Lord, saying, "Thus saith the Lord, God said to go on television with the prophetic and begin to minister."

Do you know what that prophet did? He laughed at me.

Not only did he laugh at me, but he stood in the pulpit and said, "Dixon said I should get on television and give out words from God. That sounds psychic to me."

God said to me, "Son, you have done your part, but the psychics are going to get on television ahead of my prophets."

This was a great man of God, who spearheaded one of the prophetic moves. His refusing the word broke my heart, because God said he would be a shooting star and then drop. When the changing of the guard comes, his name will literally go into oblivion. He could have filled the hunger in people's hearts for words from God that have now been filled with the psychic counterfeit.

God said, "I will do nothing, but I will reveal it to my friends. I will speak to My people, the prophets." (Amos 3:7.)

We are dull of hearing. That is why God is giving us another chance, another opportunity! It is sad, however, that too many times Christians let the world lead the way in music and in other areas. Then, although we have the real thing, it looks as if we are copying the secular.

If prophetic churches and prophetic pastors across the nation do not prepare the people for Jesus and meet their needs, there will be a price to pay.

If we do not, God's money is going to the psychics. This industry is making millions every day. Worse yet, many more people's lives will be destroyed and, perhaps, their souls lost forever.

What Is Prophecy?

What is personal prophecy? A prophecy is God releasing an anointing upon a prophet or prophetess of God to speak to your potential and not to your experience. This definition distinguishes current prophecy from biblical prophecies, many of which already have been fulfilled.

Some teach that all prophecy is simply to confirm what already is in your own spirit. However, I would say that some prophecy will never confirm. God does not have to get your permission before He does a new thing in your life.

Neither David, nor Saul before him, seemed to already know they were to be kings, nor did any others in the Bible as far as I can tell. That teaching about confirmation comes from the fact that, under the New Covenant, we have the Holy Spirit — the source of all inspiration — living within us. The assumption, however, is that everyone hears the Holy Spirit in some way or other.

Perhaps that is the ideal, but in practice, it is not the case. If we are sensitive to the Spirit, we may have a "witness" to a prophecy and think, "I don't understand it, but that *feels* right."

However, oftentimes our minds are so set one way that we do not immediately have a witness. In that case, we have to rely on whether or not we can "confirm" to our satisfaction that the one who prophesied to us is truly hearing God on our behalf.

God is a jealous God. If you come with idols in your heart, you may receive false prophecies. (Jeremiah 23:13-40.)

David said, **Create in me a clean heart, O God, and renew a right spirit within me** (Psalm 51:10).

Too many times, we have our own hidden agendas. We have our minds set in a certain direction and are determined that what we have in mind is God. If you have done this and stand before the prophet of God, and he tells you something different, you get upset with God and with the prophet!

You may then tell your friends, "He missed God." What you are really saying is that the prophet "deflated" your ego. Prophecy is to your potential, which God knows and you do not always know, and not to your experience.

God has deposited certain things within you, and as long as you are obedient and walk with God, you can receive the personal prophecy from a prophet, and it will come to pass. The key words are "obedient" and "walk with God."

It does not matter if all of the apostles laid hands on you and prophesied the word of the Lord, or the twenty-four elders around the throne prophesied to you, if you do not work with God — that prophecy is not going to come to pass.

Then you will get upset and say, "The prophet missed it," never "I missed it."

I have a problem when a prophet prophesies to ten people and hits them right on, but the eleventh person says he or she missed it. He has heard from God for all but one person? No. What that tells me is that you have an idol, a hidden agenda. You are playing games with God.

When Henry Ford began to develop the combustion engine, a lot of people did not believe in him. But he believed in what God had given him. He was a man of destiny. He invested time, energy, and money. Can you imagine, if you had the opportunity to invest into Henry Ford's company at the initial stage, how many billions you, or your descendants, would be worth now?

If something is God, I am going to jump in at the initial stage. I want to be one of the foundation builders. I want to be one of the people quick to follow God.

When Pentecost was restored at Azusa Street in 1906, a lot of people sneered, jeered, and backed away. Then in the 60s and 70s, when the charismatic ministries started, a lot of people did the same thing. But when it became popular, everyone wanted to jump on the bandwagon.

God has given us one more chance. He has given us a challenge: To fulfill the mission of the prophetic. However, we need to be taught. If ever anyone needed to be taught, it is the PIT — Prophets In Training. Untrained prophets are dangerous.

16
Prophets Must Be Trained

Before this company of prophetic people can go out preaching Jesus, they must learn to sit at a pastor's feet and be trained. A two-headed cow is a freak; so is a prophet who thinks pastors are beneath him.

If a prophet does not have a mentor, if he does not find someone to pastor him, he could very well make a shipwreck out of his life.

Nor are prophets to take the place of pastors. They are to complement, to work with, to respect pastors even after they have been trained. The enemy is angry with the prophetic move, and when prophets make mistakes, he capitalizes on them.

For example, if a prophet gets a word for his pastor, he should write it down and give it to him or her, then forget it. He should not go back the next week and talk to the pastor as if he were not on speaking terms with God himself!

Prophets should not go around introducing themselves as "Prophet so-and-so." If God wants to make you known, He will do so. Prophecy should not be considered an end in itself, but a means by which God's will and direction are made known to someone.

On the other hand, too many pastors are afraid to work with prophets. Pastors need to weep with budding prophets, to "change the diapers," to groom and counsel them. God wants the hearts of pastors and prophets to be knit together.

Pastors, training prophets is like rearing children. There will be times when they embarrass you — but do not "shoot" them for it any more than you would a child. Everyone learns through mistakes, or ought to. Let's all humble ourselves and work together to build the Kingdom of God.

The important thing is to prioritize Jesus! No matter how helpful a prophecy from God has been, do not magnify the prophet. He or she is simply a messenger, not the Source of guidance and direction.

If you are called to be a pastor, more than likely you will go to Bible school or seminary and get your pastoral training.

If you are called to be a teacher, you go to university and major in teacher's training.

If you are called to be a medical doctor, you go to university and medical school. You do not go for a one-day course and then "hang out your shingle." If you are legitimate, you do not buy a piece of paper that says, "I am a doctor."

You go through training, through strenuous training. Even after you graduate from university, you are still not a doctor. You need an apprenticeship, hands-on training, an internship.

Somehow Charismatics, when we are called, think training is not necessary. We think training is not important. If we can prophecy two or three prophecies accurately, we go to the pastor and tell him, "You are history. God has called me to be a prophet."

The Bible says in Hebrews 5:14 that we must learn to exercise our gift. When you are called to be a pianist, you do not just get up and begin to play Bach. No! You spend hours breaking your knuckles going through boring, awful-sounding scales. You do not like it. It is hard work.

Your parents make you practice, even if the neighbors complain. You work on it, work on it, work on it, and then one day you are a professional. You put on a black tuxedo with a bow tie, and when you play, everyone gives you a standing ovation. At that point, you forget how hard all the training you went through was.

It takes the same thing to become a prophet who truly hears God. We need to be trained. We need to humble ourselves. If you have a genuine call to that office, you need to sit under a man or a woman of God — and let them "sit" on you.

Untrained prophets can be moved by the flesh and the soul as much as by the Spirit. I discourage "parking-lot prophecies" or restaurant prophecies. If a budding prophet goes to a restaurant without money and sees gourmet food when he is hungry, he could be influenced to prophesy to the one who has the money whatever that one wants to hear!

No one is there to judge that word. It is not on tape. That is why it is very dangerous to the prophet and the one prophesied to if leadership is not there. Let us also watch out for prophecies given in house meetings. You eat pizza and popcorn, and the food and atmosphere can cloud your mind.

A lot of marriages began through prophecies when the Charismatic move was just getting started, and many of them ended in divorce. The word was not from God at all. Personally, I do not even prophesy to people to get married.

I tell them, "Let the romance work, and get to know one another."

After the honeymoon is over, you are going to see the real person. You are going to hear the man snoring. You are going to see how he throws his socks here and his dirty underwear there.

You are going to see how she looks first thing of a morning with curlers in her hair and no makeup. I mean, you are going to see the real person. There had better be some romance involved, some real love, not just someone's prophecy.

Prophets and Pastors Should Be a Team

A PIT is supposed to complement a pastor's ministry. Prophets are supposed to be a help and not the whole answer.

The Bible says the spirit of prophecy is subject to the prophet. (1 Corinthians 14:32) When the pastor is preaching, you can wait. He is the boss, he is the daddy, he is the man. He is the man in the limelight, the one through whom the Holy Spirit is speaking. That is God's order in operation.

If you have a prophecy and it is God, it can wait for God's timing. The Holy Spirit will not interrupt Himself through the pastor. If it is God, He will confirm it. It is not true to say, "But I cannot help myself." The Bible says you can.

On the other hand, too many of us pastors want a skillful prophet who is groomed. No, pastor, God wants you to sit and change the diapers and weep with them, and counsel him, groom him or her, and grow with that person. God will knit your hearts together, and he will be a blessing for you.

But quickly, we want to write people off, because we do not have time. A ministry gift is still an earthen vessel. Pastors, my admonition to you, my encouragement to you — please accept this as prophetic — I am begging you in the name of Jesus, work with those called to be prophets.

Work with them, speak into their lives. Build relationships with them. Give them opportunity to practice, although they are going to make mistakes, even embarrass you. However, one day they are going stand before a crowd fully matured, and you are going to be so proud.

Our children spend our money, and go to the refrigerator and eat everything. They eat, eat, eat and do not give anything back. They are our responsibilities. Just so with spiritual children. Paul wrote that the natural phase comes first, then the spiritual one. So as these "baby" prophets progress through the natural stage, they may break your heart, disappoint you, and even hurt you.

Many times you may feel like killing them! You can understand why prophets were stoned! I am serious. Many times they will open their big mouths at the wrong place or the wrong time. But please do not break their spirits.

Begin to pray and ask, "Lord, does this person have a teachable spirit?"

When they have teachable spirits, begin to work with them, begin to shape them. Jeremiah 18:1-4 talks about what a potter does with a marred vessel. The potter simply makes it over. Pastors, you are the hands for the Potter. Work with those vessels in His way.

Remember, God gave you grace, pastor. This is the time to sow grace into someone else's life, as Paul was admonishing Philemon. If you commit to work with that prophet, you will find that the love of God "has been shed abroad" in your heart for him or her. (Romans 5:5.)

Keep working to groom that one. Comb the "insects" out of his fleece, feed and water him, and give him plenty of caring attention. One day, you will realize that lamb has grown into a mature sheep. Then you will be very proud of him, and he will turn and give you the accolades. However, your greatest reward will be seeing that person grow into the potential God has for him.

When our pastor makes a mistake, we are quick to forgive, "Oh, that's our pastor. We'll just pray for him."

When the visiting evangelist misses something in the service, we let it pass.

When the teacher gets his facts partly wrong, we overlook it.

However, just let us think the prophet made a mistake, and it is "get your shotgun — boom, boom, boom!" We want to shoot him and get rid of him. Historically, prophets always have been stoned eventually, so to speak, even when they were right.

Learning To Hear God

Some people wonder how prophets hear God. Does God speak only occasionally and to special people? How can they give us the word of the Lord?

God speaks all of the time. The fact that we do not all hear does not mean He is not speaking or that there is no sound in the spirit realm. We do not hear because we are not "tuned" to hear. That is why budding prophets need to spend time with God, praising and worshipping, praying and listening.

The more anyone develops a relationship with the Father, the better you can "hear" Him, the more often you will just "know" what He wants. The Bible says those who have spiritual ears, let them hear what the Spirit is saying. (Revelation 3:6,13,22.)

There are audio and visual waves passing through the room where you are right now, for example. You cannot see or hear them because you are not a receiver for those waves. However, turn on your radio or your television set and *tune to the right channel*, and you will get reception.

God wants to "fine tune" the screens of our spirits and our minds. Jesus said His sheep know His voice. (John 10:27.) Do you know the voice of the Lord? There are three "voices" that we can hear in the spirit: God's, the devil's, or our own spirits.

You "fine tune" your receiver to hear God through building a close fellowship. When you become born again, you have a relationship, but too many Christians keep distant fellowship. A good place to start is with His Word. In the Bible is everything God wanted us to know about Him and His Kingdom.

Study to show yourself approved unto God. (2 Timothy 2:15.) Getting to know the voice of God is a daily walk. There is a price to pay, a dying to self, a setting aside of other things to make time for God.

A closer communion with God will also help you when you do begin to travel in the ministry. People will hurt you, some pastors will use you, and different ones will take advantage of you. If you have not dealt with your soul — mind, will, and emotions — it will be easy to become bitter.

Then you could begin to say, "I'm going to fix that church," and manipulate and connive, and perhaps slip into witchcraft without realizing it. Then the Lord would say, as He did to the disciples wanting to call fire down on a town that did not receive Him, **Ye know not what manner of spirit ye are of** (Luke 9:55).

One of the saddest passages in the Bible is where Jesus prophesied to His disciples something that would happen at the Judgment. He said people would come to Him thinking they were His, and He would have to say He did not know them. (Matthew 7:22,23.)

They will say, "Did we not prophesy for You? Did we not work miracles? Did we not preach and do this and that?"

But He called them "workers of iniquity" and said He *never* knew them.

"I never had a relationship with you. You had a hidden agenda and were in the ministry for your own gain or pride or lust. You manipulated people. You were doing witchcraft, not My works. You messed up a gift."

You may wonder how anyone could begin in the Lord, then slip into witchcraft and not know the Holy Spirit had left him or her. Samson did. Remember Samson? He was one of the judges of Israel before they had kings. (Judges 13-16.)

Samson did great things to protect Israel from the Philistines, but he never dealt with his flesh. The Bible says he "wist not" (was not) aware when the Holy Spirit departed from him. (Judges 16:20.)

When psychics make a mistake or blow it, no one is going to say anything. But let the prophet not cross his t's and dot his i's, you are going hear it on ABC and NBC, and who knows what CBS will say. The enemy wants to destroy the prophetic ministry, so if he can indict it in some way, he will use that to discredit the prophetic move.

That is why we need to be trained, that we will not "blow" what God wants to do. We need to be in place and in order so that we can become that prophetic company to prepare the ground, to act as a forerunner, for what God wants to do next.

I believe the main key to this is twofold: humility and love.

About the Authors

CARLTON PEARSON: Carlton Pearson of Tulsa, Oklahoma, is pastor of Higher Dimensions Family Church and founder of the Azusa Conferences and Fellowship International. Pearson is a masterful writer, intelligent, witty and dramatic. Within his presentation, you will feel the genuine spirit of the apostolic authority and fatherly, humorous teaching style that is the trademark of his ministry. Pearson unmasks the subtle deceptions of satanic influence in God's house.

PAMELA VINNETT: Pamela Vinnett of Tulsa, Oklahoma, is the founder/president and chief instructor of Prophetic Age Ministry Institute and Conferences. Her writings are scholarly and profound, but simplistic enough to instantaneously grasp and apply. The subtle reprimands and chiding of God bring the reader into an intense relationship with the Father as she ushers you into the Bridegroom's holy chambers. This author provokes you to answer the call to greatness in Christ.

MARK CHIRONNA: Mark Chironna is pastor of Higher Call Christian Center of Raleigh, North Carolina. Chironna's innate brilliance shows a unique blend of supra spiritual, practical, cutting-edge revelation. His teachings are spellbinding. His writings demand that you seek the face of the Father in reverence. Don't be amazed if you laugh and cry within the same breath.

RAPHAEL GREEN: Raphael Green is pastor of Metropolitan Christian Center, St. Louis, Missouri. His extraordinary prophetic, apostolic aptitude places him above the norm in unraveling God's deep mysteries. This author prompts his readers to study to master excellence and present God only the best in holiness and respect.

DAVID IRELAND: Dr. David Ireland is pastor of Christ Church, Montclair, New Jersey, and founder of the unique Leadership Training Institute School of Ministry. As a true apostle would, Ireland causes Jesus' grace to literally leap from the pages of the manuscript, pruning away our prejudicial self-indulgent, unethical views of forgiveness and true love in Christ. He revolutionizes the truth of God's grace.

PAULA PRICE: Dr. Paula Price is pastor of the church and apostolic founder/president of Everlasting Life Institute and Ministry, Hillside, New Jersey, a four-year degree program based on training for the five-fold offices. As an author, she is one of a kind, displaying the dramatic, pedantic, raw, down home truth about God's Kingdom and His commanding generals. You will be amazed with the revelation as to who are the true "principalities" in God's Kingdom.

CHARLES DIXON: Dr. Charles Dixon, founder of Global Ministries, hails to us from Ghana, South Africa, initially, and is currently of San Antonio, Texas. This author is quite learned and lends correction to the erroneous doctrines so long exploiting the Body of Christ concerning the ministry of the prophet. Though he cuts deep like a surgeon, the anesthesia of God's love deadens the pain. His teachings will lift you to another level of understanding in Him.